THE SOULFUL STRIPPER

EAT PRAY HUSTLE

MERCEDES MICHAELS

First published by Ultimate World Publishing 2019
Copyright © 2019 Mercedes Michaels

ISBN

Paperback - 978-1-925884-69-2
Ebook - 978-1-925884-70-8

Mercedes Michaels has asserted her right under the Copyright, Designs and Patents Act 1988 to be identified as the author of this work. The information in this book is based on the author's experiences and opinions. The publisher specifically disclaims responsibility for any adverse consequences, which may result from use of the information contained herein. Permission to use information has been sought by the author. Any breaches will be rectified in further editions of the book.

All rights reserved. No part of this publication may be reproduced, stored in or introduced into a retrieval system, or transmitted in any form, or by any means (electronic, mechanical, photocopying, recording or otherwise) without the prior written permission of the author. Any person who does any unauthorised act in relation to this publication may be liable to criminal prosecution and civil claims for damages. Enquiries should be made through the publisher.

Cover design: Ultimate World Publishing
Layout and typesetting: Ultimate World Publishing
Editor: James Salmon

Ultimate World Publishing
Diamond Creek,
Victoria Australia 3089
www.writeabook.com.au

Dedicated to my daughter, mother, family, friends and all the beautiful souls I have met along the way. I couldn't have done it without you.

In loving memory of my dad xx

Disclaimer: The following book is an autobiography of some of the main events in my life that have shaped me. They are as I remember and experienced them. This recount is simply a telling of experiences through my lens. I understand that others may have a different view of events. I have changed names to protect people's identities and intend to cause no harm to others reputations. This is my life, my story and my perception. I hope you enjoy it.

TESTIMONIALS

"Mercedes believed in me and helped me find the confidence to pursue something I've always wanted to try. I'm so grateful for her consistent encouragement and support that is both loving and firm. Mercedes is an authentic, down-to-earth, powerful, brave and gentle woman. Her guidance has enabled me to express and explore my creativity and sexuality, which has led to improvements in my health, finances and relationships. Thank you Mercedes for changing my life."

– **Chloe Fairway**

"Mercedes is a real inspiration. Her love for helping people and the passion she shares for co-creating deep connections with her clients is what makes her a fantastic coach. Strongly recommend her services for anyone wanting to learn how to let go and live their fullest and happiest life!"

– **Shane Blackett** www.yogainthevines.com.au

I had followed Mercedes' journey for over a year and had reached out to her before to let her know just how much she had inspired me on my own journey. A year later I was urged to contact her again and it didn't take me long to figure out why. Mercedes has an amazing presence and ability to hold space for her clients. Her ability to gently guide and encourage her clients towards their truth whilst also offering other insights makes her an incredible life coach. I have immense gratitude for the work Mercedes is doing.

– **Trish Porter**

ABOUT THE AUTHOR

Mercedes is a lover, mother, author, mentor and action taker. With a huge open heart and the tenacity to believe in her dreams she inspires others to achieve theirs. Whether in her coaching practice, her personal relationships or in her work environment she strives to be her best and bring out the best in others.

By fully owning who she is – the good, the bad and the ugly – it gives permission to others to live their fullest expression of truth.

CONTENTS

Testimonials v
About the Author vii
Introduction xi
Chapter One: Challenging Childhood? 1
Chapter Two: Miss Understood 11
Chapter Three: My Seductive Secret 23
Chapter Four: Super Sydney 37
Chapter Five: Uganda, Europe, and Beyond 47
Chapter Six: Do you need a visa? 59
Chapter Seven: My Shining Light 73
Chapter Eight: Baby and a Backpack 85
Chapter Nine: Our Gypsy Adventure 93
Chapter Ten: Supercharge your story 103
Offers 119
Speaker Bio 121
Acknowledgments 123
Images 125

INTRODUCTION

As my Great Aunty always says, every story begins with Once Upon A Time. And I can't think of a better way to start this one. You see, this is a story that's been wanting to be told for many years. But there were many aspects about my life that I couldn't accept, and I didn't think that anybody else would be able to accept them either. It's safe to say that it's taken a long time and a lot of inner work to get to the point where I am ready to share my journey with all of you.

I'm sharing for many different reasons. One, to help others. Two, as a form of therapy. And three, to inspire others to be able to step into who it is that they truly are. I really believe that all of our journeys begin way before we come to this planet, or way before we're born into the physical realm. It's my belief that we bring in patterns and wounding from our parents, their parents and so on. I am also of the belief that we experience more than one lifetime each life, that we get an opportunity to heal just a little bit more of these patterns and peel away a few more layers of the onion to eventually reveal more of who we truly are at the core, which is love.

CHAPTER ONE

CHALLENGING CHILDHOOD?

So, here goes. Once upon a time in The Granite City of Aberdeen, Scotland, a beautiful baby girl was born – okay so maybe scratch the beautiful part. I was apparently more like a skinned rabbit for the first few months of life rather than a bouncing baby girl. I was born in August 1983 to my mother Marilyn (whose ripe old age of 25 was considered a geriatric pregnancy) and my father William. My parents had tried to conceive for some time and when I was born they were over the moon.

My mum comes from a lower working class background in the suburb of Masterick. My grandparents on her side were hard working and like most people in Aberdeen my grandad worked away at sea a lot, leaving Grandma to juggle five children and two jobs – one as a fish wife at the fish factory and the other as a home carer. Times were tough with seven living in a two bedroom house, with my mum's eldest sister taking on the role of mother for her four younger siblings. My mum was the youngest girl and had one younger brother.

Like many Scottish folk booze and being merry was a way to escape the perceived hardships and the cold. Booze, in fact, was the remedy for many a thing! Baby's teething? Rub some brandy on it's gums. Baby isn't sleeping? Put some sherry on the dummy. These kinds of things were the norm in the 80's in Scotland – well at least in my family!! It's safe to say that I was introduced to alcohol in some measures as a very young girl and it has continued as a theme throughout my life.

My dad had been an only child to a beautiful dark haired woman named Margaret and his father was named William as well. It seemed to be the done thing in that era to give your children your name. I don't remember too much of what my dad told me about his childhood. He spent a lot of time out in the countryside, in the village of Mintlaw, with his uncle and grandparents…and from what I remember him sharing he managed to get up to a fair bit of mischief. They had been from a more affluent background but still fell in the range of the middle class. My dad's mum fell ill and passed away when he was just 20 – although she never smoked a day in her life, she was riddled with cancer. My grandad went on to remarry and until recently I was quite unaware that they were step family! To me they were what I knew to be my family and in my younger years we spent a lot of time together. I get the feeling that my dad never really got over losing his mum and there certainly wasn't a culture around then that encouraged people to share and feel their emotions. So he dealt with things the way he knew how and that was through drinking, partying and suppressing. My dad was not really an angry or aggressive drinker but more the life of the party. For those that know me it's definitely something I have inherited!

Anyway, now that you have a little background about where I have come from it may set the scene for how my life has unfolded to date. Back to my parents and here they are – fresh bundle in arms, neither particularly prepared for the challenges that lay ahead of parenting. Like many new parents realising that parenting doesn't come with a manual or a manuscript, they did the only thing you can in that situation – wing it and try your best!

For most women in Aberdeen, it's kind of the norm to expect your partner to work away a lot, either on a fishing vessel or on an oil rig. My dad worked on the oil rigs in the North Sea, and he would spend months or weeks at a time away…who knows, maybe it was less than that, but it always felt like an eternity to me. The women tend to click and create really close bonds with their families and young ones. In my younger years, I obviously don't remember too much, but what I do remember is a lot of joy, laughter, family outings, vacations, day trips, and I feel like my mum really tried to make up for the absence of my father. I would say in the early days, my mum and dad had a pretty good relationship, but I can tell she must've had a bit of resentment growing because she was stuck doing the hard yards with us and the minute my dad came through the door it was like my mum didn't exist. Not long after I turned three my sister showed up – let it be noted that I was particularly unimpressed at having to walk whilst she was in the pram and even more so to share the spotlight of my parents' affections!

We were particularly close to my mum's family. Seeing as she came from a big family there were always plenty of kids around of my age that I could play with. I had many really close cousins growing up and we were always in and out of each other's houses, playing in the woods at the back of my house and riding our bikes in the streets in the days when it was "safe" to do so. Every Sunday, someone would take it in turns to go play cards at their house. Kids would run amok, the adults would drink, play cards and bet. It really feels like the slogan "work hard, play hard" was the motto for life! My life was routine, comfortable and predictable – just the way I liked it.

I was around seven and my sis was three when I started hearing talk of this place called Australia and that we were going to be moving there at the start of the next year. I feel like it all happened quite quickly, from hearing about it to moving. At the time, everyone in Scotland were huge fans of the TV shows Neighbours and Home and Away, so there was one part of me that actually thought I was going to be on TV. I actually thought I was going to move to Ramsay Street or to Summer Bay, because in my seven-year-old mind, that's what Australia was. I remember kids at dancing saying, "You're so lucky. You're going to move to Neighbors." Or, "You're going to have pet koalas and kangaroos," as though they just hopped down the main street. There was that part of me that felt excited about the new adventures, but there was also a part of me that deeply longed to keep the connection that I had with my family. I didn't realise until actually writing this book how much that really meant to me to feel connected and to feel part of something – I was slightly petrified of the unknown, but nevertheless, a few months later, our house was packed up and we were ready for our big adventure.

That Christmas, my aunty threw a massive party, the sendoff of all sendoffs. We had a lovely Christmas dinner with all the trimmings, everyone was dancing in the living room, there were party hats, Christmas crackers, and I'm pretty sure we were dancing to something Kylie Minogue inspired. My cousin, myself, and my little sister Kristie were all in matching outfits and having the time of our lives, not really knowing what was to come.

That was the last Christmas we spent in what I knew as my life. On January 1st, 1991, we upped and moved to Australia. I remember flying, my sister and I in matching shell suits, down to London. I distinctly remember my sister's god-awful screaming. She had had something wrong with her ears on the plane, and she was just a mess. When we got off the flight we were hurried through Heathrow to find the medical centre to get a clearance – I remember a blur of bright lights and yellow high vis vests. They were not going to let us get on the next flight to Singapore.

Anyway, something must have worked out and her ear must have popped because we got on the next flight. We landed in Singapore, and for the time being, it was still like a holiday. We enjoyed rooftop swimming pools and swim up mocktails at the bar and shopping trips with Mum. And we had a few days there to settle in. Then we transitioned down to Perth, and it was so hot. I had never experienced anything like it.

We'd left Scotland, which was literally snowing, to come to Australia, which was in the high 30s and early 40s at that time. I just remember thinking, "I may die here." You see, houses back then in Australia, they weren't built for the cold, and they weren't built to cope with the heat either. So, they were these hot boxes with, if you were extremely lucky, maybe a little ceiling fan to help move around the hot air. In those moments it felt like a version of hell, so far outside my comfort zone.

We had arrived in the school holidays, with plenty of time to get used to the idea of our new life. We'd checked out the schools, but it still felt very much like a holiday. Dad was off work, everyone was…it was all pool parties, barbecues and excitement because we'd never done these things before – going down the beach, learning to boogie board. These were all things that previously happened once in a blue moon when you were on a holiday in Spain somewhere.

Knowing they were going to become part of our real life was actually quite an exciting thing. So, amongst all the new houses and schools, we got settled and went about our new life. After a few months at my new school, I was beginning to feel the loneliness and separation. I had a thick Scottish accent that I was teased a lot for. I was sick of feeling like an outsider and, so desperate to fit in, I began to consciously adjust my accent for school or home. I am sure I am not alone in this feeling when moving school or country!

I used to have these thoughts about wanting to find an island that I could live on that was smack bang in the middle of both places so that everyone from Australia could visit me and so could everyone from Scotland, but that I distinctly didn't want to make any new friends on the island because then that would create even more people to miss if I moved again. I struggled with the feeling of heartbreak that I wouldn't be able to see my extended family whenever I wanted. It affected me so badly that I made a promise to myself that as soon as I was old enough I would return to Scotland.

If I scan back through my childhood and I think about the things that really shaped me as a person and that really either made me better or gave me issues or whatever it was, there are a few main things that stand out from a hazy childhood. Although I want to take this moment to really express that I don't feel like I had a "bad" or "horrific" childhood by any stretch BUT like any human experience there are moments that make us, shape us and break us.

I remember one time going to the Christmas pageant and being in a lift, in a glass lift above the pageant. And all of a sudden, the lift stopped. And I remember this man standing next to me saying in a joking tone, "You better not breathe because we'll run out of air." Because of this one simple saying, to this day I will still sometimes hop out of a lift before the door closes because I will just have this wave of panic fly over me, and likewise with locking doors in small spaces, float tanks and scuba gear. It's like I am okay until I'm not okay! So, I really challenge myself and put myself in small places to try and break free of this, but I have got some level of claustrophobia linked to this one sarcastic throw away sentence. Even now as an adult my mind knows logically that it didn't mean anything but my body has stored the fear as a kneejerk memory. It has also made me hyper aware of the power of our words, even the ones your own little internal critic tells you about.

The next thing that really shaped me was the divorce. My parents, they made it a few years into being in Australia together. But I think the lack of support and the lack of friendship around them began to show the cracks in the relationship. My dad was always working away, and my mum didn't have great support in raising us. I can hazard a guess she was homesick, trying to figure out who she was and where she fit in this new country and then on some level resenting my dad. What happened to the grass being greener?

My dad, like most Scotsmen, liked to dabble in the drink. Again, the motto "work hard, play hard" comes to mind. I have flashes of hearing my parents arguing when we were in bed, "Just come home to your family first, come and see the girls before you head to the pub!" These words have always stayed with me, this sense of not really feeling chosen. And yet, I can see in my logical mind that my dad didn't really have any coping mechanism for the high stress of his job nor did he have any tools for raising or being part of a family either.

After the divorce, my mum's lack of physical presence had a big impact on me. I know in my gut that she was out there slogging away doing whatever it took to keep a roof over our heads, to keep us dancing, to keep us being able to go to as much as possible and for those sacrifices I am deeply grateful. At the same time, the little girl inside of me just wanted her to have the time to be with us.

The last thing that I've realised had a major effect on me was this: I remember we had family friends coming out to visit, and it was so exciting to have people come out from the UK and stay with us. And I remember I was maybe seven and a half, almost eight at the time, and the family friend, who will remain anonymous, was maybe about 13. My sister and I were into playing tag, fart jokes and pulling people's pants down – as a seven year old, it was completely innocent.

One night after going to sleep up in my loft bed (the kind that had a closet and desk below it), this family friend came into my room and switched on the light.

"Come down here, come down off your bed," I was a little startled because I didn't know what was going on. I couldn't see him at the end of my bed and recall going down the ladder thinking, "He must need something." Instead, I just saw this fully naked boy/man, with a massive erection. It's the first time that I'd remembered seeing any male anatomy. The way the room was set up with the ladder at the end of my bed and the door being quite close I found myself back against the wall and feeling cornered. He was so tall and strong for his age, I could feel my heart racing and my blood pumping.

Not really knowing what was happening or where to look I recall this feeling of my body going into complete contraction and just not being able to breathe. He was quietly saying to me, "I want to hug you and kiss you." Something within me knew this was wrong and pushed me to get back up the stairs and onto my bed, saying, "No, I've got to go to sleep now." I tucked myself in but could not sleep. I just lay awake staring at the ceiling for what seemed an eternity, fearful that he would come back in the room. Just before he switched the light off and left the room, he said, "Don't tell anybody. Don't tell your mum. I'll send you money for your birthday." That was the final moment, and although this "incident" was never spoken about again between us it played on my mind for years and years to come. I then somehow connected sexuality and sensuality directly to a monetary value, which also explains a lot about the industry that I have chosen to pursue.

For many years I brushed this to the side feeling that because I wasn't raped or touched it wasn't "that bad" and yes, by comparison this wasn't the worst thing that could happen but it is all relative to your perception and previous experience…"not that bad" still caused me to feel petrified around my own dad. But I did not say a word, I didn't even dare mention it to my mum until six years later when I went into a complete meltdown about going on vacation back to Scotland. I don't know if she was in shock but other than saying I wouldn't be left alone with him, nothing was ever mentioned again. I kept this all bottled up, and I swallowed it and I made stories about it in my head. I had huge anxiety about many things. And it has actually been one of the major things that has impacted my life and relationships with men as a teenager and now as a young woman. I'm not going to say that I'm grateful, but I will say that to some point I have come to a place of peace with the person and I can have compassion and understanding for where they were at as a pent-up pubescent boy with no real guidance on what to do with it. It's really a big belief of mine that to reduce incidences like my experience we need to be educating prepubescent boys and girls on what to do with this newfound sexual energy and hormones, to open the communication shedding guilt and shame around talking about sexuality. I hope through discussing my experience to make some leeway in this area.

Without wanting to discount my experience nor dramatise it, aside from the above I feel like I had a relatively normal childhood. I had hobbies, I danced, I was fairly well adjusted. And by this stage, I'd made it through primary school in Australia. I'd found my clan, and was feeling super excited to move into high school.

CHAPTER TWO
MISS UNDERSTOOD

Well, my previous excitement about moving into high school may have diminished when I actually arrived there. High school was a game changer – all of a sudden I was a small fish in a huge fucking pond. It's also where I learnt my love of swearing, a way to vent some of the anger and anguish that was now fueling through my pubescent body. If my swearing is going to put you off reading the rest of this, then I'm sorry, not sorry. We just may not be each other's people, which is something I've come to totally accept. If you're able to skip through the swearing in this book then I would love you to… there may just be one little gem you grasp that adds to your life or helps a piece of the puzzle fit.

There was something partly rebellious and partly conformist about swearing. Part of me wanted to go against the teachers, against the rules, to break free of the chains of my strict mother. The other part of me wanted to fill my desperate need to belong in my new environment. The group of girls that I'd played with in primary school were now strewn throughout the varying popularity groups. I remember initially I sat with a new bunch of kids from all kinds of schools. They were the A group – the cool kids, but I was the silent dorky one within the group.

Always on edge, always feeling anxious, not quite knowing what to do or to say to be accepted and cool. A lot of these girls were more well developed than me – they had interest in boyfriends and guys chasing them. In contrast, I was still this scrawny little boobless thing that was, to put it simply, really bloody awkward. This awkwardness would go on to become somewhat endearing and something I grew fond of…coining myself later in life Awkward Bambi. All legs and no social co-ordination.

I would sit there and try and pick up a few things, try to use their lingo, dress the right way, steal some of my mum's makeup after she had gone to work in the mornings. No matter what I did I just couldn't ooze "cool" like the other kids. Eventually I found myself most comfortable moving into the group that was kind of top of the C's, bottom of the B's – if we're going by grades. So, here I was in this new C group, which was a mixed bunch. There were people from all over and from all walks of life. And again, although they were now my new buddies and we did everything together, there was still a part of me that felt lonely and isolated. I still felt like an outsider and having a strict mum didn't help me win points in the popularity contest. One girl in this group is still my best friend to this day though, and my life would not be the same without her! I will share more about her later in the piece.

It was quite common for me to hear the words said about me, "Oh, why are you hanging out with her?" Or, "Oh, don't invite her." On reflection it's interesting that because I felt isolated, I then attracted these situations that mirrored exactly how I felt inside. I was very insecure and I wasn't really too sure about my place within the school. So, aside from putting makeup on the way to school, and maybe buying a little padded training bra, I didn't quite know what to do to fit in! Then by a stroke of what I thought was genius, I started stealing my dad's cigarettes to sell them as a way to make money for canteen – or to give them away to the cool kids so that I had a reason for them to like me. This went on for a while and I began to gain some traction with my plan, although inevitably I took up smoking too so I could hang with the cool kids in the toilets at lunch and recess.

You must've been able to smell it from a mile away. And quite often, teachers just turned a blind eye. They knew we were going to do it anyway, and quite possibly they smoked too. To look at me, I was tall, gangly, skinny, flat chested, had a pretty face but was pretty much a plane Jane as I'd consider myself. I had many nicknames. Anna, Steggles (which is a brand of chicken), Chopsticks. I hated them all. Anna was short for anorexic, of course. I remember one guy saying to me, "Hey, you better walk with your arms out in case you fall down an ant hole." Back then I really had no inner knowledge of who I was or my inner beauty, or anything like that. As a result, the external judgements of others became my gauge for how good a person I was.

I never liked to wear a school skirt. I always liked to wear pants because I was really paranoid about how skinny my ankles were, feeling that my feet looked like big boats dangling off the end of skinny ropes. One day for sport we had to wear netball skirts and the feeling of dread that washed over me was enough to send me into panic! So that I could take a look at my legs in a waist high mirror, I stood up on what seemed to be a chair with four legs. Unfortunately, the fourth leg was bent inwards, and just as I put all my weight on it, the chair tipped out from under me and I landed flat palmed with all of my body weight on top of a straight arm. Surprise, surprise, I broke my elbow. This is where my mum gave me the nickname Vanity Smurf – she was amazed I was so vain as to look in a mirror, and break my arm. There's a bit of a standing joke in my family about that now.

High school on the whole for many kids is a semi-form of hell. Whoever came up with the idea of uprooting kids from the comfort zone of primary school, while they're simultaneously losing the comfort of childhood and how their body used to be, has a lot to answer for! It's torture – well that was my experience at least. Being so awkward and insecure meant that I required a shitload of external validation to reflect any that I had going on in the inside. It took me so long to learn to love myself for more than this. If you are going through this please just keep swimming towards the light, there is magic to be had on the other side of your own self-acceptance.

At school, things were okay I guess. I was settling in my new group, but I was put in a new form – they had the bright idea to mix some really bad kids in with the "good" kids in order to hopefully help the naughty kids out. I was one of the good kids and the only thing it did for this insecure little thing was to make me try to prove even more how cool and back chatty I could be to the teachers. This resulted in me having interschool suspension, low grades and a fuckload of attitude. Looking back I just wish I had actually paid some attention and put the work in – compared to adulting doing school work was easy!

Since my parents divorce things had been tough at home. I can only now see exactly how hard it is to adult when you are struggling to make ends meet, keep a house running, raise "wilful" children, juggle school and work schedules, then actually try to have a life of your own. Quite often with my mum juggling being at work I was looking after my sister for the few hours between school finishing and her getting home, which meant that for the most part after school hangouts were out of the question. I also wasn't allowed to have other kids come to my house as my mum didn't want to be held responsible for anything that happened when she wasn't around. As an adult I can see the logic in it all, but as a young teenager trying to figure who and where she was in the world it felt extremely unfair!

My mum had been dating some guy for a little. He was nice enough, but they were from different walks of life, and all of a sudden she started dating the brother of her best friend at the time. It all seemed to move really quickly. He was kind, generous and charming. After struggling on her own and her last boyfriend being a bit of a snotty prick, I can only imagine the feeling of relief and lust that must've powered the streamlining of their relationship. They sat us down and talked about him moving in and it being a trial basis to see how things went. Initially it was going to be a one month trial. I agreed to it, thinking, "I'm glad that they've asked me. And yes, if it's one month and if things go ass up, he's out."

Things were great for the first few weeks with the new boyfriend, let's call him Tim. Tim was extremely generous with his time, skills and helping out financially around the place. As he got more comfortable and complacent in the home, though, he started to throw his "energetic" weight around the place. It was mental how volatile and opposing his moods could be and you were never quite sure what would trigger him. At this stage there was a total misunderstanding between my mum and I, and Tim had never had any kids of his own before. It was like the blind leading the blind in retrospect, not to mention throwing in two pubescent, reactive teens. It was never going to be an easy transition but holy fuck it definitely didn't need to be as difficult as it was! Now, let me tell you a little bit about Tim. He'd come from a strict Irish Catholic upbringing, where he'd been belted around the head for being insolent, until the age of 14 when they found out that he was actually not insolent but instead completely deaf in one ear. Very much the Irish family, where everything was swept under the rug and it was all about keeping up appearances. Nothing was spoken about, everything was shameful, and everyone just placated each other so as not to upset the balance of what was really going on. Later in life many things came out within the family resulting in his own brother being sent to jail for molesting his own children!

Needless to say, Tim had a shitload of repressed anger – so much so that it would explode, and when it did there was never any warning. You couldn't find a trigger specifically. Anything could set him off, and when that happened it didn't matter what you said, he was just in another world. He became demon-like and there was no way of contacting the generous, loving version of him – somewhat remnant of Dr Jekyll and Mr Hyde. My mum, sister and I began walking on eggshells, we would tiptoe around him trying not to do the wrong thing. The issue with that was that because we never knew the trigger it made it an impossible task. Life became very stressful and strained.

Tim was a painter, like a house painter, so as you could imagine his shirts, even when washed were covered in splats of dried paint. This one time, I was folding the washing and I couldn't actually tell which side was the outside and which side was the inside of the shirt. I innocently thought, "I'm going to make this look really nice and folded so that he's happy with me and everything will look neat in the drawers." So I did the buttons up, and I folded the collar back, and folded it so it looked like it would if you'd seen this shirt in the Polo Ralph Lauren store or something like that. A few days later he went to put the shirt on from his drawer, and all hell broke loose. In his mind, I had done the buttons up and turned it inside out, on purpose, to make it harder for him to get into. I can only imagine this concreted the idea in his mind that we didn't like him, and validated his story that the world was out to get him. In hindsight I can see how he got that idea, but the fact is he didn't ask me, he just flew off the handle. My intentions had been purely innocent and had, in fact, been an attempt to gain some praise from him.

My mum was at work that day and Tim was in charge of looking after myself, my sister and three of his nieces and nephews. We all had known each other for some time as our mums were best friends. They were all quite a few years younger than me, ranging from 5-10 or 11. I can't remember exactly how old I was at the time, but definitely between 13 and 15. I was supposed to be allowed to go out to my best friend Candice's house that day, and I was so looking forward to this rare flash of freedom I was now being allowed. Candice is one of those people who just got me. We seemed to bond over having the strictest parents in the world at some stages. At that time, she had moved out from her dad's house and had way more leniency with her mum. We were virtually inseparable in the years that followed, to the point my mum questioned my sexuality with her. I have been lucky enough to have this girl in my life to this day, we are each other's certain type of weird. Friendships like these, that can stand the test of time, are few and far between and I am always grateful for that.

Now back to the moment at hand! Mum was at work, Tim was in charge and he had just had an Oscar winning meltdown about the fucking shirt. This resulted in him cancelling my "playdate" – I'm not sure if that's still what they are called when you're 14, but you get the drift! This meant the end of my world as I knew it, so I stormed into my room, slammed my door and put my CD player on – at the time I was playing Iris by Goo Goo Dolls on repeat. I had just got the CD from my boyfriend at the time, my first holding hands and having a little peck on the cheek boyfriend. I had probably slammed the door behind me in a complete rage myself. In my head I was thinking "You're not my dad. Fuck you. Who do you think you are? I'm going out! I haven't done anything wrong," while also feeling really upset that something I'd done in an attempt to please him had actually angered him to this point. Thus emerged the people pleaser complex I have worked so hard to shake later in life! If I felt that someone misunderstood me or was unhappy with me it would affect me to the point of not being able to sleep. It rocked my confidence to the core.

Not long after he came and ordered me out of my room. He thought I should be "social" with my newfound cousins who were all sitting around in the living room watching a movie. He told me again that I wasn't to go out that day, so as a hormonal, rebellious teenager, I was pissed. I sat there sulking, crossing my arms in a huff and muttering under my breath. This enraged him further and he flew over toward me and got right in my face with this gnarling, passive aggressive, derogatory tone in his voice.

He started pressing his three fingers into my forehead, tapping them repeatedly as my head bounced off the wall behind me. "You little fucking idiot." He did it over and over, his mouth and warm breath hitting my face as he spat venomous words toward me in front of everyone. Feeling shocked and belittled, I rebelled and I went and sat in my room, blasting my CD. The next minute, the door flew open, and he proceeded to rip the CD player out, pick me up off my bed and throw me down on the carpet. At the time, I was wearing a pair of high-waisted Levi jeans with the wide flare bottoms. They were all the rage. He grabbed the end of my jeans and pulled me along the carpet, leaving a massive graze up my back.

I had put my hands out to grab all the doorways whenever I had a chance, cutting the tops of the jeans right into my hips till they bled in the process. I don't exactly remember what happened next, but I was a mess. I didn't want to be in that house anymore, I didn't feel safe and I had never seen him react to this extent before. I had to play smart, so I calmed myself as quickly as possible.

"You can go back into your room so long as there's no music. That's your punishment." Result! As soon as the coast was clear I snuck out of my window, went around the opposite side of the house, and climbed the fence. My heart was pounding and thoughts were racing as I dashed across the front of the house – what if I didn't make it in time before he caught me?

I remember running, and running. By this time, I was over an hour late to meet my friend so she was out for the afternoon, and at that time mobile phones were still for the few. I arrived at her house shaken and in tears, as her mum sat me down and let me get it all out. I felt like I could tell her anything. She knew that I'd smoked and so she offered me a cigarette to help me calm my nerves. As I puffed away I was shaking my head in disbelief at what had just happened, feeling so misunderstood, and so trapped by this situation that was our new life. That was it! I would tell my mum and she would kick him out and life would go back to normal! Or so I thought...

After telling my mum nothing seemed to change. This is by no stretch an aim to shame my mum at all but Tim had gotten to her first, he had emotional manipulation down to a fine art and he made it sound like I was just an insolent teenager, that none of what I said really happened nor was it "that bad". So, when I shared with my mum, she already had the watered down version in her head, or maybe she wasn't quite ready to deal with the fact that this guy was so emotionally manipulative and abusive. It didn't help my case that I was a rebellious kid and I can see how this all worked in his favour to create separation between my mum and I. It was to the detriment of our relationship – the less and less she spoke up about these things, the more and more it enabled him to feel like he had the right to fly off the handle at us.

I remember being so confused and misunderstood at times that I set up an appointment with the school chaplain to try to wrestle my mum away from Tim's twisted grip. I will never forget her saying when we left the appointment that I was never to embarrass her like that again and that it was American bullshit that children had input. Parents were parents and kids were kids. I can understand now that being unappreciated for everything she did do for us and crucified for what she didn't do would have been deflating, but in my eyes I really felt I had no other options left.

I ended up being the one who would challenge him, speak back to him, and attempt to protect my mum and sis. I know for sure Mum caught the brunt of it behind closed doors and was dealing the best that she knew how. Some big part of her liked the idea that somebody else was in control and she didn't have to figure it all out for herself – single mumming is exhausting. On top of that she wanted to see the good in him – remember I said that when he was good, he was great. He was kind, he was generous, he was loving. But we just never knew when this Doctor Jekyll would come out from behind the clouds and dampen any occasion. You could guarantee that almost any big event would be ruined because he'd find some reason to create explosive drama around himself. If I could describe him in one word it would be volatile.

This kind of a relationship slowly chipped away at my mum's self esteem and her worth. It was awful to watch, because my mum had always been a strong, fierce, independent woman. With every confrontation she became less and less sure of herself. At times, her friends influenced her, saying, "Well, when the kids move out, who are you going to be left with? And you don't wanna be left with nothing or no one." I guess they still come from a generation where being alone is way more tragic than being miserable. In their defense he was very good at putting on masks so people would question if he could really be that bad. On reflection I can see how he did that. Again, this is all my perception and my assumptions. This book is a recount of my version of events, which have all built towards me becoming the woman I am today!

My mum and stepdad, as we called him even though they were never officially married, were quite strict. My mum was a little bit of a catastrophist, liking to catastrophise everything. In her mind if I went to an underage disco for 12 to 18 year olds, there would definitely be an 18 year old wielding a syringe that was full of drugs and HIV, and that I would get stabbed and contract it. World War 3 was guaranteed to begin at any party that I went to, and I was definitely going to die in a pool of my own vomit. Very fear-based parenting but I can see now that it was her version of love. I have often thought that fear-based love is counter intuitive – you see I still found ways to sneak out, to lie about my whereabouts and go to these events (although not as often as I had liked). It was just now my mum had no way of protecting me or making sure I was safe!

I feel like this kind of upbringing built quite a few character traits that are really great for me to have in my life now. It built resilience, it built the ability to look at problems and find a solution. If I couldn't get to the party by asking directly, I had to get creative and find another way to get there. You see, things that may appear negative on the surface always have a positive side, depending on the way you allow yourself to view it!

Okay, now where was I?

Ah that's right, boys! In the midst of all this craziness happening in my home life, it's really odd that I managed to secure a boyfriend. What interests me is that I'd found myself my very own controlling, aggressive ticking time bomb. My first boyfriend was a Macedonian man (by this stage we were both 16) who was very similar in demeanour to my stepdad. When we were good it was amazing, but when it was off, it was awful. A very tumultuous, volatile first relationship in retrospect but at the time it was all I knew so I thought it was "normal". He was my first, the one that gives you the feeling you can't breathe without him. I thought it was love, but it was more co-dependency. He had a car so he was also my way to stay away from home for as long as possible. Around this very same time, I changed high schools, got into modeling, and also found out the most earth shattering news…my dad was ill with cancer. The man I had looked up to and put on a pedestal my whole life was sick, and I just didn't know what to do with myself. This was around the same time that I discovered alcohol, so all of a sudden there was this medicine that could help me either feel emotions that I couldn't feel otherwise, or suppress ones that I couldn't cope with. This magical medicine that allowed me to just drink away my problems, but at the time, in my head I thought I was just enjoying a great social life. I had a great school life at my new school, finally being one of the popular girls, and I was still dodging bullets left and right at home.

We had squared off, gotten physical, walked tightropes of emotions trying to please this bastard, and my mum was so worn down by this point that she just seemed saddened by everything. We had even attempted family counselling, but to no avail. His evil side began to take more of the spotlight, and I could tell when looking into his eyes as he had me pinned down by my neck on the table that there was a tortured little boy inside him. He was screaming in my face "I want to hang you over the edge of a cliff until you shit your pants." He was spitting and flushed scarlet as he seethed the words at me through gritted teeth. My mum to this day denies ever hearing of this incident.

The final straw came when he wanted me to get up off the couch and do the dishes one morning. I had been out the night before and had Candice staying the night. I had explained that we were finishing a movie and would be done in ten minutes, and at ten minutes on the dot, he came back in and abruptly switched the movie off. I rebutted, "We've got to return that! Just let me watch 15 minutes as I can see the end is near." The old VHS was a guessing game. Well, that was it. He went crazy.

"You said you'd do it in 10 minutes. So, let's go." Grabbing my arm and screaming right in my face like a corporal in the army. Well in that moment something snapped, maybe it was because I had extra courage with my friend there. I got right in his face and I spoke to him the exact way that he had spoken to me. It really took a lot for me to get to the point where I spoke to him like a piece of shit, I was usually too scared – not this time. He flipped out at my reaction pushing me flying through the air, slamming my back against the wall and as I slid to the floor my top came down, exposing my newly budding breasts. I must've been about 16 at this point, a very late bloomer and now embarrassed as all hell.

I saw red, feeling violated and having had enough of years of his bullshit. I flew towards him. On the way I had picked up a Tupperware heavy microwaveable pan that had been sitting on the washing basket. I smacked it over and over his face. He stood there like a deer in the headlights for a few moments but then I saw the rage begin to bubble. Candice had just got her drivers license so I screamed, "Get your keys!" and we ran for the door. I have never moved back permanently into my "family" home ever, ever again. Though I was only 16, I feel like this was the end of my teen years, the end of my childhood.

CHAPTER THREE
MY SEDUCTIVE SECRET

Over the next two years I bounced from short stints at my dad's, friends' places, boyfriends' houses, to occasionally renting rooms. I hated not having a place to call my own. Struggling financially to get on my feet I found myself floating between temp jobs and working low-end part time jobs in ice cream shops and the like. I even found myself working in a butcher shop at one point! I didn't last long there – the guys used dip their chain mail gloves in pales of blood and thought it was funny to wipe it down my arms, or better yet, chase me around the shop with ox tongues and try to lick me with them!

Like most kids my age I was partying hard, and on this one particular night, in the wee hours, I find myself sitting at a table in the middle of a strip club. There's tacky silver sequin curtains, red carpet that sticks to your feet, cigarette smoke and dim lighting. All this excitingly intrigues me, as I shyly peer at the women dancing for men on the podium. Something about this felt "naughty", like something I should hide away. I never ever thought I would have what it takes to do what these women did. I had been sitting with a bunch of male friends and after a few drinks I had relaxed into these surroundings when a girl came over to our table brimming with personality and confidence.

I started asking her a few questions about the ins and outs, and the more I heard the more turned on I became and when she disclosed the earning potential I was sold! Sugar, her working name, had what I wanted! Sass, confidence and above all cash!!!!

Side note: at the time I was dating my high school sweetheart. We had met in final year but danced around, not actually becoming boyfriend and girlfriend until the night of my 18th birthday. He was an amazing guy, tall, dark and handsome with the purest green eyes. He was hurt by the fact that I was interested in starting in this industry. I have held a torch for him for most of my adult life actually. He was the one that you wished you had met in your late twenties instead of late teens. I was so in love with him and he with me, that all in kind of love…I was scared that he was my forever so I freaked out and pushed him away. I let the lifestyle and the job come between us. I broke his heart and shattered mine.

For me, it wasn't only the money that enticed me. There was something about this dirty little secret that drove me wild. I wanted to know more about this adult playground. I wanted to know more about this bunch of misfits that somehow made a family. The allure of money and the fantasy side of things seemed like the perfect escape. I was feeling nervous, excited, exhilarated. And for the first time in my life, I actually felt alive.

I quit my $7/hour job, got my first lease on my own little place and began dancing at the Dollhouse a week later. I remember my first night so clearly. The week prior I'd made friends with the DJ and this other girl, whose dancing name was Sky. They came and picked me up – I remember his little cool blue convertible car, and I squished into the back seat with all of his speakers and the likes. Sky and I were downing Sambuca and wine like it was going out of fashion, and on this night it didn't even touch the sides. My nerves and adrenaline had taken over any feeling that would allow me to lose control and get drunk. I wanted to take the edge off, but nothing could.

The best advice given to me was to just get up on the first pole at eight o'clock, because no one would be in there yet. We had to be on the podiums in case somebody did walk in. So up I hopped in my tiny little black dress that I bought for a modeling competition years earlier, with my hair scraped up and a clip on pony tail, in the hope of maybe deflecting my true identity on some level. I danced around shyly not really knowing what to do. Alas, a man walked in. He was wearing cargo pants, and a T-shirt with a zip-up jacket. He sat down, his belly resting on his thighs, slightly overweight and out of shape. I sat down on the glass podium, and shuffled my way towards him, like I'd seen the other girls doing. I moved and touched my body in a way that was foreign to me, and after a few moments I very nervously held out my garter around the thigh, not quite sure if I had done "enough" to earn the dollhouse tipping money inside my thigh, and then I danced some more.

My friends were in the background cheering and egging me on and showing me what to do. I was extremely lucky that this particular gentleman was a regular. He wasn't too harsh or too judgmental about my stuttering nervousness. Something happened the more I moved sensually and I felt good, like really good. I held my garter out again in a way of teasing more money out of him. I danced and I sat on his lap, rubbing my hand across the top of my dress, slowly peeling it down to reveal my pale, perky dd's. The look on this guy's face was amazement. This was new to me as I had been a late bloomer, only growing boobs in the final year of high school. I felt like I was finally being noticed and appreciated by the opposite sex. There was something really satisfying in the way he looked at me and the knowledge that he couldn't have me.

Before I had to go any further, my turn on the podium had come to an end and I thanked the man and walked off into the change room. The coming months would bring many bottles of champagne, many, many customers who I inevitably friend zoned myself with, and lots of money. I had definitely been burning the candle at both ends. I was in the toilet one night and said to one of the girls, "How do you girls drink, stay awake, dance and hustle all night? I'm dead on my feet!"

"We have a little bit of this," one said as she passed me a little baggie of white powder. "Just put some on your gums. It'll absorb really quickly into the bloodstream and you'll feel amazing." The little white powder was speed. In my mind I thought it cant hurt, so I said, "Okay, cool. Let me try." I was so naïve, I rubbed it into my gums and under my tongue, and in the next ten minutes I felt superhuman! I was oozing confidence; I loved this version of myself that gave no fucks. I was soon sitting in the middle of a table of saying, "who's next for a lap dance, get out your wallets boys." I morphed into this alter ego, a money hungry woman in charge. Inevitably, this is what changed the dynamics in my relationship with my highschool sweetheart resulting in our break up. I let the money, control and compliments go to my head.

I had entered some competitions that had been held at my home club, and shot a lot for the club's marketing and advertising. I thought by wearing a gangster hat or an eye mask I was basically camouflaged to the rest of the world and that no one would recognise

me! My pictures were plastered on the top of cabs and I was soon to be published in the Exotic Angels Nude Calendar. My guilt and shame were starting to get the better of me. Although I loved and fully owned my new life within my work space and a few very close people, I had gone to great lengths to keep what I was doing hidden from the public and my family. In the end I wrote a note to my mum telling her about my secret life and left it on her pillow. I spent all afternoon pacing up and down waiting for her to storm me. I was so anxious about her response that I called the landline and asked if she had found the note. When she eventually did read it she said, in a disapproving tone, "When are you going to tell me you are a lesbian, or pregnant?" as if to ask how much more could I disappoint her. We already had a very touchy relationship and this just put more gunpowder in the cannon.

So, here I am earning all this money (for back then), trying to figure out how to run my own household and pay bills on time, whilst simultaneously getting fed copious amounts of free drugs and alcohol. I didn't even realise that I had a job. To me it was just one big party. Life became working at the club, rolling into another club, rolling to

EXOTIC ANGELS — MISS SEDUCTION AUSTRALIA 2002)

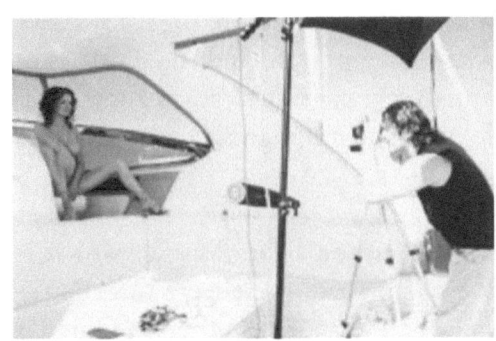

the casino, rolling home, sleeping till the afternoon and getting up and drinking a bottle of wine as I got ready for another night of it. Now these bottles of wine obviously made my head hurt and made me feel like crap. So, hand in hand with them would go another little pick-me-up, another little bump that would get me through the evening.

In the midst of all this I met Jake. Jake was the older brother of a boy in my year who I thought was the most charmingly irresistible man on the planet. He was this dark haired, tattooed, chisel-faced gorgeous man that all the girls loved. Little did I know that he had a huge drug problem. He had recently stopped injecting speed, so instead we started snorting a shitload of it. In my head it was much better as at least he wasn't shooting up. And our whole life became work, drink, chase, repeat. By chase, I meant chasing some more drugs. I couldn't see the point in going out to a party or to work if we didn't have drugs. There were points there where I wouldn't get out of bed without a line next to it.

Around the same time I had met Jake, I had been planning to move back to Scotland. I needed to see if going back would refill the emptiness I had felt since leaving all those years before. I was also starting to get really bad comedowns, beginning to feel like I didn't want to be on the drugs anymore. I was starting to see the effect, the sparkle that it was taking out of my eyes. Jake and I were only supposed to be a bit of fun in my mind, and after one particularly bad bender, where I thought he was going to die of an overdose, I told him I loved him, and that was it. He chased me over three months later to Scotland. And we began working and living there together. After some time in Aberdeen we moved to Edinburgh, and the illusions of family life were shattered. Although it was great to see my family, it wasn't like it was before. People had grown up, grown apart and life had gotten busy.

Edinburgh was amazing. We moved to the Grass Market which is right below the castle. At the top of the road, there were three "strip clubs" within a triangular distance of one another, otherwise known as the Pubic Triangle. They were like family pubs that randomly had strippers in them. I started working at one pub and Jake worked behind the bar in another. I never really meshed or gelled with the club that I worked at, The Burke and Hair. So, after a month or so I moved over and we worked in the same place – The Western Bar.

For the most part, it worked okay, but it definitely brought up a lot of issues in our relationship. Him physically seeing me work was quite destructive. That's where I really had my eyes opened to a whole new world, being in this environment where many friends in the club and behind the bar were heavily tattooed, self-expressed and covered in piercings. It was a world that I had been sheltered from living in Perth. I remember sending photos back, getting them printed and my mum stressing yet again that I'd now, God forbid, become a lesbian. These friends were just open-minded. I felt accepted for who I was in that moment, and what I did. My friends became my family and I have such fond memories of my time there.

Some of the girls and I somehow got invited to perform and form a troupe for the first sex exhibition, Festival Erotique, in Edinburgh. This was a fairly groundbreaking thing – bear in mind that it was 2002 – and we performed a fairly "out there" show, doing a little bit of burlesque style, jazz, erotica and BDSM pieces. It was like a taster show of different aspects and ways to tease and experience sensuality. When I left, the rest of the group went on to tour with this sex exhibition through Europe and Scotland for years and years to come. It was a really exciting movement to be part of, bringing sexuality to the forefront, to the "public" forum and out of the shadows. I felt completely okay doing this as I didn't know many people in Edinburgh and there was no such thing as social media then!

At around the same time, Jake proposed to me. I'd felt obliged, I guess, in some ways to say yes, because he'd followed me all the way over there. And unfortunately, as much as I wanted it to work, I just kept thinking about my ex and how I shouldn't have left him and how I'd quite abruptly cut him out of my life. I tried to push this down in a way and I tried to make things work with what was realistically quite an insecure and paranoid partner. The drugs had created a lot of psychoses and paranoia for Jake, and it really played out with men in our friendship circle and with customers – things became quite volatile. I felt in some way that I was trying to grow and leave the drug scene behind and even though we weren't actively using he just couldn't shake the paranoia. He couldn't evolve past where he was. So, when we left Edinburgh, I gave it a six-month trial in my head for him to get things together or it was over.

In between being away, and all of these happenings, my dad was still ill. I guess me burying my head in the sand and becoming part of this other world was a way for me to escape the pain of what was really happening. I carried a lot of guilt and shame around not being able to be there for my dad during his illness. Often, now, thinking about him sitting there lonely and scared at night with this awful illness, I just didn't have the tools or knowledge to cope with the emotions that were swirling through me. Seeing the man that I had put on a pedestal my whole life deteriorate into a Golem-like creature as cancer tore through his body – it devastated me.

There were so many close calls. I remember being on a nightclub floor in Aberdeen and getting a phone call that my dad had to go for brain surgery, and literally going to the airport from the nightclub to fly home and try to be with him. When I got there, I just booked work because I couldn't be around him. We couldn't have a conversation because it was stuck in both of our throats, what we knew might possibly happen very soon. I am glad I that I finally plucked up the courage to be able to apologise and say, "Look, I'm so sorry that I've been away. And I'm so sorry that I've been in the next suburb and unable to visit you because I've been coming down off drugs or drink benders, because I just didn't know how to be around you."

He was able then, after I shared my feelings with him, to open up and offload some of his guilt and shame around being away for most of our childhood as a result of the divorce and working on oil rigs – for not seeing more of us. We both kind of came to an equilibrium, this understanding that we both felt the same way, and also knowing we truly, deeply loved one another. We both found it hard to see the other one suffer. I took so much solace in that conversation, which has always led me to believe that we need to have difficult conversations. It's so important to say the things that you really want to say regardless of how that might affect the other person, because you might actually uncover something that is really therapeutic or helps you process something that you've been thinking about for a long time.

Jake and I got back into the drugs. I'd started at a new club, and this became a new family. One thing that I've always found was that whenever I've been at a club for long enough, there's always a real family connection. I don't know what it is – maybe the fact that we're a bunch of misfits that has finally found some way to belong and be understood? I've always felt like the strip club is family to me, and I know that sounds really weird. Something about the vulnerability of being naked with people. It's like you just cut through the bullshit, and all that's left is who you are.

By now I'm really back on the drugs pretty hard. I have a new bestie, Heidi, and she is still a long time friend to this day. My drug use was pretty bad, and so was my dad's health – he deteriorated and deteriorated. I had been at a party one night – and we'd gone all night – it was now the morning and we were trying to call someone to drop off more drugs. My phone kept ringing and ringing and ringing, I kept hanging up until I noticed that it was my mum's number. She kept ringing again and again to the point that I just answered it. I said, "Yes," and she says, "You need to go visit your dad today." At this stage, he was in hospice care. I brushed it off saying, "Oh, no, no, I'll go tomorrow." Her reply was, "There might not be a tomorrow, it might be too late."

Those words, they struck me like a freight train. I couldn't move, and I couldn't speak, I didn't know what to do. I turned around to the group of gaunt-faced party goers that were left as the sun was coming up, and they just knew something was wrong. I dropped my phone and went blank. I don't even think that I could get a tear out. I was stumped. Jake called a friend of ours who had been at the party the night earlier and had only drank to come pick us up and drive us down to the hospice. Sitting in the car on the ride down, hearing the chatter in the background, I was on another planet – like I was watching a movie of my own life. I was looking out the window at the sea sucking on an icy pole, which is a godsend to any druggie on a come down.

I just couldn't believe it. I couldn't hear what anyone was saying. Everything was muffled. I felt like I was on the other side of the glass from everybody. When we got there, my dad was doped up to the eyeballs…he wasn't with it at all. Occasionally, he came to and said something. The last thing he ever said to me was, "I want to take you for an ice cream." To this day thinking about that chokes me up, even as I write this the tears are rolling down my face. While I'm at his side, I keep needing to run to the bathroom to dry heave at the stress and the drugs leaving my system. Night fell and finally I fell asleep on the couch in the spare room. In the wee hours I sat bolt upright from my sleep. I just had this feeling that I needed to go and sit by his side.

When I sat there, looking at the clock and hearing his laboured breathing, I remember thinking, "If you don't go soon, I'm going to go get the morphine myself and put you out of your misery." There was a part of me that felt so guilty for even thinking that, but part of me felt like it was only fair to him and to everybody else. Not long after, his breaths became fewer and farther in between, until finally, they just stopped. I woke my mum and my sister up off the floor, and they came over to the bed and my mum went over to hug him, even though at this stage, they've been separated since I was ten. She really was helpful when he was ill. He took one more little involuntary breath, and that was it – the man that I had admired my whole life was gone.

I cant remember if I cried that day, it was like I was in so much shock I couldn't feel the emotion fully. It took me years to begin to process the grief from my body. I felt so guilty for not being able to cry, that day I lost access to a part of myself. I have worked hard to regain my softness and vulnerability.

It was no longer my dad lying on that table. There was a twisted Golem-like stone statue. It was one of the most awful experiences of my life. Only my dad could get me to laugh from beyond. We went to the casket viewing and the funeral home had shaved him leaving only a moustache! My dad had never had a moustache in my lifetime, I couldn't help but have a giggle. His death spurred me to change things – I was coming down hard. I was in a relationship that I didn't want to be in. I had decided that if life was going to be shit it is going to be really fucking shit. I broke up with Jake, and poured myself into study. I began studying makeup and personal training, eventually deciding I needed a fresh start. Ahhh, a fresh start, that's exactly what I needed!

Along with this attempt at planning my fresh start came the fear and anxiety about being found out, about the kind of person I had been

THE SOULFUL STRIPPER

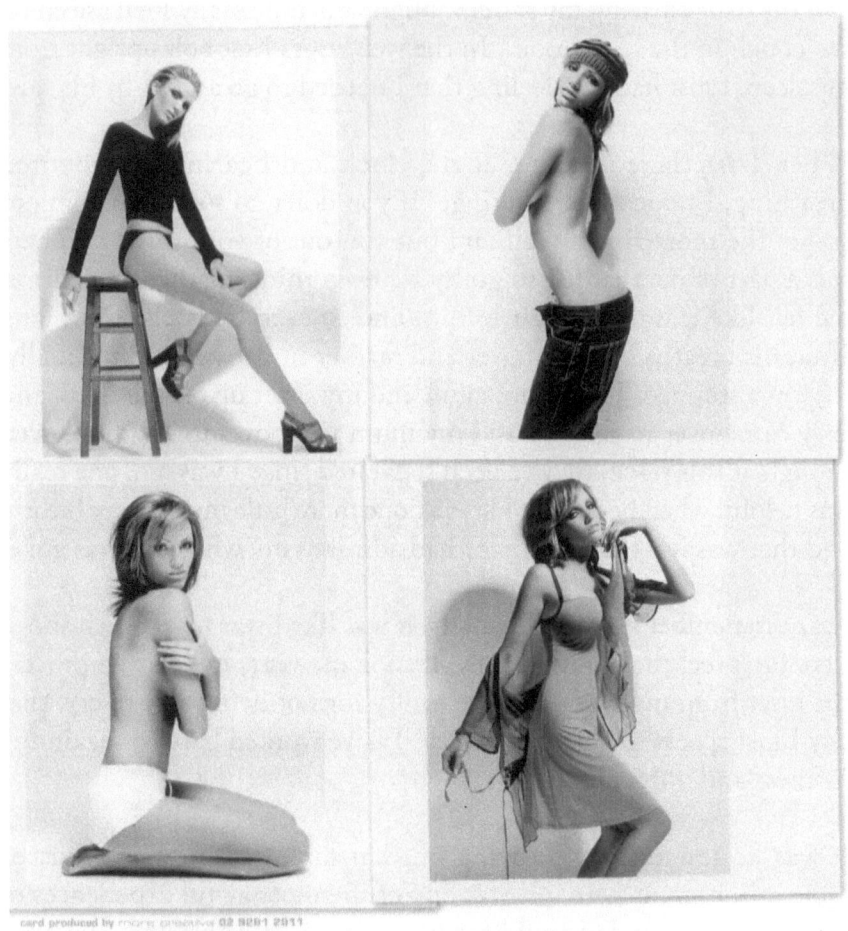

height: 5'10" **bust:** 34D **waist:** 26" **hips:** 36" **dress:** 10 **shoe:** 8½-9 **hair:** dark blonde **eyes:** blue

Level 1, 872 Hay Street Perth, WA, Australia 6000
Ph: 618 9486 9994 Fax: 618 9486 9995
email - bookings@scenemodels.com www.scenemodels.com

for the past few years, for the kinds of things I had done. So as I was trying to elevate my modeling career, I almost went into a form of self-sabotage where I would just play small and would lay awake at night with such anxiety about someone finding out my dirty little secret? What if someone found out what I did? I had this sense that it made me the worst human in the world. Perth is a pretty small town and although I had some okay modelling assignments I was always holding back. I needed to be somewhere where no-one knew my face that would open me to new opportunity. So that was it, I was going to the big smoke – Sydney. I had this grand idea that I could reinvent myself, which I did to some extent but the funny thing with moving is that you take yourself with you. I carried the same internal dialogue wherever I went, the dialogue about being a bad human and having to hide my true self away.

It wasn't until I could truly own that piece of me (that would come many, many years later) that I was able to really be proud and enjoy my job. It's actually been a very recent thing that's become available to me through looking at my "stuff". The journey inwards has really allowed me to know who I am, what's important in life and accept that it's okay if someone judges me. Generally others judge through ignorance or because it's a reflection of what's going on for them, and it's not really about me at all.

As you can see this was a really fucking awful time of my life. I felt like life couldn't throw any more at me. I had no option but to rise and recreate. Here we go, Sydney bound...

CHAPTER FOUR
SUPER SYDNEY

I'm not exactly sure why my pattern is meeting men just as I make huge life changing decisions, but here I was doing it all over again. With Jake well out of the picture and a severe inability to be alone at this time, I had met a guy called Owen. This union was like two stars colliding – it was dramatic, deep, magical, explosive and volatile. We were the blind leading the blind in this thing called life. I was deeply broken by the loss of my dad and he was broken by his parents' divorce and some other personal things he had going on. It was the kind of 'can't keep your hands off each other' lust/love, fuelled by boozey, drug-filled nights and stupid arguments. Not little, quiet arguments, but the slamming doors, storming off from parties kind. We were the epitome of a love/hate relationship – such a fine line we tread but at that time in my life it was what I knew to be deep love. It was the only version I had ever known. So, as crazy and dramatic as it was, he was mine and I was his.

So this is all happening at the same time I had decided to move to Sydney, and I said to Owen, "If we are still doing this when it's time for me to go you are welcome to come with me." I just knew in my heart that I needed a fresh start. I was aching to get away from all that reminded me of my dad, somehow feeling like that would make things easier.

As I mentioned I had been trying my hand at some modeling in Perth but was never confident enough to fully step into it. I also had a regular gig as a Marilyn Monroe impersonator, which was always a blast! So there I was in the pits of my devastation with a newfound will to rebuild myself. I had reached out to my booking agent in Perth to see if he could hook me up in Sydney. My agent was a tall, bald man in his 40's, as camp as they came. I remember him saying to me in a drawling tone whilst looking down his nose over his thick-rimmed glasses, "Well darling, if you are going to move to Sydney you will need to look at losing an inch all over."

With my external and internal worlds a complete shambles, this came at a point where I needed something to focus on, and it got me to the gym more. I was already studying to become a personal trainer, but where this failed me miserably was that I felt like I wasn't good enough unless I hit those measurements. My self esteem was at an all time low and I began to OBSESS over calorie counting and exercise output. Reflecting on this time I can see that I was using this newfound addiction as a form of control.

Obviously, I didn't know that this was what was playing out at the time. I was just overwhelmed with thoughts like, "Oh my gosh, I need to hit this weight. I need to lose these centimetres. I need to be an inch smaller, pronto." It would get to the point where I would eat something and write how many calories it had in it and then cry and try to recalculate them. Maybe that wasn't classed as a medium apple, it could have been a small instead? Then I could have more calories. Maybe that steak wasn't 200 grams but instead 150. Anything I could do to try find an extra few calories in my very strict 1,100 calorie a day regimen. I was probably the thinnest that I've ever been, I was looking amazing, yet I was the most unstable and unsure of myself I had ever been. I spent hours in front of the mirror looking for the outfit that would make me appear the tiniest bit thinner.

I remember throwing whatever was in my hand at the time at Owen if he were to eat pizza or chocolate in front of me. I mean, how dare he? If I couldn't have it, then he shouldn't have it – what a complete prick for torturing me! I can see the insanity in all this now and have a laugh at it but at the time I was so deep in my obsession I couldn't see beyond my next meal.

God forbid I would drink too much and be tempted by McDonalds on the way home. I remember sitting down inhaling a Quarter Pounder whilst simultaneously sobbing with guilt that I was eating it! I felt crazy, but I couldn't stop.

I had finally hit my goal measurements, and I was so proud of myself as I headed in to the modelling agency. I thought I was about to get praised by my booker – again desperately seeking the validation I needed externally, but instead all I was met with was, "You could probably lose another inch all over"! I was devastated. I think I binged so hard that night I ate an entire family pizza and block of chocolate myself. I was in utter disbelief. When would I ever be enough? Around the same time, I was told that big boobs would not get me anywhere in the modeling world. I was currently a 10e on a size 8 frame. If only my boobs were smaller then things would be okay. I tried to fix myself on the inside by tweaking the outside. I had a breast reduction. The peace I thought I would find in fixing myself from the outside in never came. Instead it caused huge rifts between Owen and I, as he couldn't understand why I would "massacre my body" as he put it.

You know the funny thing, I then didn't get chosen for a job that had previously booked me every year. The client's reason, you ask? I was too thin and had lost that sparkle in my eye. By luck it was exactly what I needed to hear. It didn't completely end my weight obsession but it definitely put things into perspective. It was the first time I caught a glimmer of the message that the right people, clients, and friends will love you as you are.

Back to Owen and the impending move. Owen had never been out of the state and although things weren't amazing he agreed that he wanted to come and give this a go with me. We worked super hard on getting the money together and getting all the i's dotted and the t's crossed so that we could get over there soon. By this stage I was half-living my new gym life and half-still-living my old underworld life…I kept allowing myself to be pulled back into the party scene. After Owen and I made the decision to move things got worse. Until then we had enjoyed a fairly crazy, experimental sex life, but all of a sudden that stopped and my advances were denied, bringing up a whole new level of rejection for me to experience. I felt the shift, like a plug being pulled out of the wall. My soul couldn't feel his soul anymore and it killed me. The silence was deafening, I was alone but clinging on to try to bring back what we had. I ignored it all, hoping it was just a phase and off we went to Sydney.

We ended up settling in the little town of Cronulla, a beautiful, perfect, summer bay-esque little town where you can run along the cliffside, swim at the beach and shop at all the little cute boutiques in the street mall. We thought this was going to be our happy, that this was going to be our place, but again, the cracks deepened in the relationship. I had managed to set up quite a successful personal training franchise at Miranda Fitness First. I was doing really well for myself. supplementing almost what I was earning stripping through my work as a PT. I was so passionate and dedicated to this and I felt I finally had some worth and purpose. Unfortunately, for Owen, things went the other way. He went into work as an apprentice sparky and was earning $200 a week. It took a toll on his self-worth and yet again I had ended up being the bread winner.

This became quite an issue and both of our unhealed emotions started coming up. He started pushing me away by being really mean about my appearance or things that he knew I was insecure about. He teased me about having a big nose so much I almost went and got a nose job! Luckily the surgeon talked me out of it. He was just reflecting back to me my own lack of inner worth by saying things out loud. The further he pushed me away, the needier I got. We fell into the typical push/pull pattern. I knew I deserved more but felt that having someone was better than being alone. That is, until one night I got home from work, went to give him a kiss on the cheek and he jerked away from me. I just said to him, "I'm your girlfriend. I'm not a disease" and asked if he really wanted to be here as I wasn't putting up with this anymore. I went out with the girls that night, and he offered to come and pick me up. I turned to the girls, saying "See, he's coming to apologise and pick me up." Boy was I wrong.

He came to pick me up and break the news that he couldn't do this anymore. Now, not only was I in a strange town with little support, but I was now without my main person, without my comfort blanket, without the person that I thought that I wanted to be with forever. Owen moved out a few weeks later and I got myself a little place in the heart of Cronulla. Automatically my intention was to find somebody to fill the hole because I didn't know how to be on my own. I physically couldn't be on my own. I just didn't know that it was an option. It brought up all the parts in me that I needed to look at but wasn't ready to see. Fairly quickly, I laid eyes on a guy in the gym. Now, this guy was very charismatic. He was a little younger. I was 23 by now and Jude was 20. He had just recovered from leukemia and was in remission.

We were both trying to find our way into this healthier lifestyle through being personal trainers and eating healthy, yet still being young adults and going out partying – trying to find a balance between the two. Because we went in so quickly to each other, I became very co-dependent and placed a lot of pressure on him to be my person. Although he had grown up there and had his own friends and activities that he wanted to do, I became like a leech and made him responsible for my happiness completely. If he didn't invite me to something, I would go crazy and make him feel guilty. Things were messy at times, and for the most part we did everything together.

My PT manager at Miranda Fitness First reminds me of the saying "when the student is ready, the teacher will appear". Adam began teaching us not only about the physical aspect of health, but about mental and spiritual health in the way of manifesting, meditation, presence and the power of now. These were all things that were new to me. Jude and I really started to dip our toe in these teachings and see if we could make our relationship better. We started to manifest. After watching The Secret for the first time I wrote a list on a piece of butcher paper in the middle of my bedroom wall. One of the things on my list was that by August 2004 (or 5), I would have $5,000 cash. At the time, I had no foreseeable way that I could access this money. Saving it through my job or whatever wasn't an option. It would literally need to fall from the sky, so I just kept reciting my affirmations and trusting. I had no reason not to trust as I had no previous experience of this working or not working.

A few weeks later a friend sent me a link, saying "Why don't you enter this modeling competition. There's a trip for two to Hawaii as the prize."

"Oh, yeah. Cool. That sounds good." I called and I got the last spot in that weekends heat of the competition. There were heats then semi-finals and quarter finals. Anyway, finally, I make it through all of the rounds, from 77 girls to the top ten in the Grand Final. The Grand Final was on August the 4th. We had done our parades and were all lined up across the stage. Kris Fade was the MC that night and as he was pumping up the crowd my nerves were off the hook! He announced third place, then second, and I thought, "Well, there goes my chance of winning because they never pick three brunettes." My jaw literally dropped when they called my name as the overall WINNER. What happened next was even more jaw dropping! Kris went on to say that not only was the winner (me) to receive a trip for two to Hawaii, but also $5000 spending money!! I became a believer in the power of manifestation, the power of being present and self development. There I was, August 4th 2004, with my $5000 dollars.

This experience boosted my confidence and trust in many ways. I had realised that swimwear modeling was what my body type was more naturally suited to, so I began to embrace my curves and the learning to trust the universe allowed me to start experiencing more joy in my life. I also went on to win Miss Bondi! Prior to this I would be sitting on a beach but totally stuck in my head, stressing about how I would pay rent and make my mortgage repayments on a little place I had bought the year prior in Perth (oh yes I like to load my plate to the brim haha). But things didn't stay this way for long.

Not long after we got back from the trip to Hawaii, we were walking through the shopping mall and Jude said to me, "I've got to tell you something."

"Okay." I said. "Do we need to sit down or what's this about?"

"No, no, no," he said, as if it were no big deal. "I think I'm going to Canada."

"Oh, cool." I replied. "When are we going?"

"No, I'm going on my own, indefinitely."

I felt like the whole shopping centre was going to collapse on me. It was happening again, I was being abandoned. I couldn't breathe. My mind was racing, trying to make sense of things. We had been so good? He had been so into me, he looked at me in a way that no-one ever had. He told me I took his breath away and that we would get married one day…had this all been lies? I felt betrayed, I became a victim. HOW COULD THIS FUCKING HAPPEN TO ME AGAIN?!!!!

All of the trust in the universe I had felt before fell completely by the wayside, I was a bag of skin, bones and anxiety. We had ended things but he wasn't leaving for a few months, so I had the torture of seeing him at work and socially at clubs. He was everywhere – we occasionally even hooked up only to have him retract the next day. I stupidly kept going back in the hope of luring him in again and changing his mind. It was an awful time. At my worst the anxiety of life became so bad I had to sleep in the bed with my flatmate at the time, Christina. She became my rock, we did everything together.

It got me to thinking, "Is all of this about a guy that I dated for eight months?" Surely this can't be the case. It was then I realised that since my dad died, I'd gotten busy. I'd gotten really busy. I moved. I avoided. I escaped. I just got so busy with being busy that I never felt that crushing pain that was throbbing inside my body. That's what brought up that feeling of not being able to breathe. It was pure panic and a massive anxiety that had started to uncover itself in my day-to-day reality. Until then I would let a few tears fall after a few wines and that was my way of dealing with grieving my dad. Around the same time, I started reading about how to not just manifest material things, but how it all worked, why it worked sometimes and not others etc. I started reading books like *A New Earth* and *The Power of Now* by Eckhart Tolle. He spoke of his own desperation and anxiety in a way that I could completely identify with. I wasn't alone, these books became my lifeline and showed me how to turn things around.

Whenever I felt anxious, I would just pick up a book and flick to a chapter or a page to see what it said on the pages. It would always be something I needed to hear to bring me to some level of peace. I vowed then that for a year, I would not get into relationship with a man. That I would not chase it, that I would not, even if it was Brad Pitt that fell in my bed, I would not get into a relationship with another man because I needed to figure out how to be on my own. This was really tough to start with, but I started, again, reading more books and getting hypnotherapy to help me move through some emotional issues. I read and was deeply inspired by the book *Eat, Pray, Love*. I came out of a meditation one day not long after reading that and the message was clear: Oh my God, I just need to get over myself. I actually have to go and help someone that is really in need.

Thanks to a couple of well-placed conversations by the universe, I found myself a spot volunteering in a babies home in Uganda. That was it – I had no idea how I was going to make it happen but I booked my tickets. I set myself a deadline and I was out of there. No turning back now. I ended up doing a fundraiser with the help of some of my contacts in the modeling industry to raise money to take over and buy supplies needed by the home – things like mosquito nets as malaria was a killer over there, nappies, clothes and food. The fundraiser was held at Hugo's Bar in Sydney, in one of the pockets of the bar. Hugo's was very much the place to be seen in those days. Randomly enough, because we had a roped off area it attracted some celebs chasing a quieter spot to have a drink. That night I met Bryan McFadden, Liev Schrieber, the drummer from Grinspoon and Daimon Downey from Sneaky Sound System. What a night! It was my last hurrah and my mum even came across for the weekend!

There I was with my huge backpack at 24 years old ready to fly off to Uganda ON MY OWN. I had done little to no research about where I was going or what to expect, I just took a leap and trusted. I had a long journey ahead but I finally felt alive again! I still missed Jude and I still experienced anxiety and loneliness at times, but now I felt equipped with how to deal with what may arise on my journey.

Lions and tigers and bears oh my!

CHAPTER FIVE

UGANDA, EUROPE, AND BEYOND

I arrived in Kampala, Uganda, having left Sydney and my story of being a broken-hearted little girl behind, and ventured out into the big wide world to see what it's really like to be broken-hearted. What suffering really was, in an attempt to put my own pain in perspective. Firstly, let me say that Uganda was nothing like I had imagined. For some reason, I had an extremely ignorant, uneducated view of Africa, all based around poor people with their hands up waiting for food in the red dirt. I was really mentally prepared for being in the middle of nowhere, so it was much to my surprise that I found myself in a bustling, busy, semi-cosmopolitan city in some aspects. It was really busy, and there were plenty of other tourists around – or Mzungu's as the Ugandan people like to call us, which is kind of a loving taunt with maybe a little insult in, it, depending on how it's said to you. It is loosely translated to "white person". In the smaller towns outside of the centre, little kids would run down the street chasing our car, squealing "Mzungu, Mzungu, Mzungu." It brings a smile to my face just thinking about that right now – their huge white smiles brimming from ear to ear.

Needless to say I was super underprepared for what to expect aesthetically, and as a city, not knowing what was going to be available to me there, I was also very underprepared for the emotions that it would bring up in me. Yes Uganda was a bustling place, but it was also still very poor and a lot of people were in need of the basics to live from day to day. I was challenged deeply by seeing the poverty and yet not being able to do more to help. The only thing I could do was to make an impact where I was going to be volunteering, so I decided to give it my all.

I must say, although I was in part on my own version of an eat, pray, love journey, I look back now feeling a little embarrassed at how underprepared I was. Although my intentions were from the heart it also fed my ego in a way: look at me, I'm helping the people. I don't know if that was actually happening or what I thought others may think of me for going. It's all beside the point now but it felt important to mention. The other part of this experience was life changing and deeply, deeply healing. It put a lot of things in my life into perspective.

You know, previously I mentioned that I couldn't sit on a beach without stressing about how I was going to pay my mortgage and my rent at the same time, yet here I was seeing such poverty, people living hand to mouth. The difference was that they seemed to find the joy in everything, and always had a smile on their faces. Seeing and absorbing that over the next few months really was medicine for me. There is also a deep sense of community, something which our western world seems to be lacking dearly. This medicine is something that I have bottled and taken a little piece of with me. I now administer the same medicine to my clients, often encouraging them to find a way to get back and give back to the community. To share in our happiness and our challenge, to give and receive and truly feel needed is some of the best medicine there is.

Okay, now where was I? That's right, I had just arrived and was working at Sanyu Babies Home. They had an onsite volunteer place where you could stay and the money went back into the orphanage. Inside the there was a babies room, a toddlers room, and a tiny newborn babies room too. They were all split up into different sections, with the tiny, tiny babies in one little cozy room where they were watched by a certain staff on duty, and all the babies that couldn't walk yet in another bigger room, with the biggest area left for the toddlers. After the kids reached the age of four, if they were not adopted, they would move on to another children's home.

I personally had a deep and eye-opening journey whilst volunteering at the babies home. I became a part of their daily lives. I would help in the "classrooms" during the day. I was taught certain exercises to do with some of the babies by a passing occupational therapist, I assisted in meals, bath and bedtime routines. It was very much like a conveyor belt process – line up to be washed, then dried and clothed, then put in your cot. The house mama's there did a great job, but lacked the time or space to give a lot of individualised attention. This is where the volunteers came in, but often the same few kids were paid attention to – the "cute" kids. I always tried to share my love with the few that never got much. There were a few ill and disabled babies that were rarely touched or picked up by the house mama's. I was told it was because there was a local belief around them being "cursed". I don't know how much of what I was told is truth and how much was heresay. I have since had my eyes opened to a different view point and the word Voluntourism, which occurs when certain organisations that claim to be helping those in need are instead bankrolling by keeping children looking unwell, undernourished and in need. When buses of well meaning tourists come by such places and are heartstruck by their situation, then they are likely to give more in the way of financial donation. More often than not it is said that a lot of that money does not actually go towards bettering the children's quality of care but instead to lining the pockets of the organisation and it's partners.

This all got me questioning how, in fact, we can help by leaving a positive and sustainable impact. All I can really say is that when we go into an orphanage, stay for a while, create a deep bond with a child and then leave, with another tourist replacing you not far behind, are we acting in the best interest of the child? It's something to think about before going and physically helping babies. All of these little short-term connections may create a lack of ability to truly bond with someone when they do find a family, or they do get into a relationship later in life. The main thing that I can say is research where you go. If you want to volunteer and give back really research the institution, or the NGO, or whoever it is behind it. Really look at like their values, and really ask "Are they walking their talk? And are they putting their money where their mouth is? And, really, on a ground level, are they helping the problem? Or are they just band-aiding it?" A friend I had met out there has started her own foundation and is doing great things in Uganda, she runs Child's i Foundation and their mission is to see every child end up in a loving home.

Yeah, that's my little side note. Quite often I'll go on tangents, I'm a bit of a tangent queen, so I'm going to pull you back into the story. There I was, hustle, bustle, motorbikes, which they call Boda-Boda, flying past me kicking up dirt, dust and smog into my face. It gave me the total and utter feeling of being in awe, of feeling alive. It was almost like when I had previously been on the stage. I could see colours more brightly, and I felt this sense of such a deep appreciation for life. I was fully present and therein lies the feeling of aliveness, which can in fact be accessed from anywhere on the planet! The feeling was so contrary to how I had felt in my life prior that I can now identify with having experienced deep anxiety and depression.

Back home I was always watching people wondering why the fuck they were so happy. What are they seeing that I'm not? I felt like I was always sitting back, and watching the world go by like a movie, a movie that I wasn't cast a role in. I didn't know what they were drinking, or what pill they were taking that could allow them to enjoy getting up, walking with their dogs, and being nice to their neighbors. I always wanted to recluse and isolate. The only thing bringing me out of my shell until now was the drugs and alcohol

I made many good friends in town, both internationals and locals. There was just something about being there, letting go of my pretenses I'd collected in the west. This left me open to adventure of all sorts. I met some local international medical students who I went on a safari tour with and saw the amazing Elizabeth Falls, and took boat trips down the Nile to see crocodiles three times the size of me! One of the most amazing things that happened to me when I was in Uganda was having the pleasure of being asked to be on a local TV station. One of the guys that I met at the orphanage, he was a little bit of a free TV local celebrity, and he took me down into the slums where people welcomed me into their homes, all the kids came running out to greet me, screaming Mzungu, Mzungu. I got the opportunity to interview them, and they would interview me, and they'd all have the same four questions that they had learned in English. They'd say, "Who is your mother? Who is your father? What is your job?" And then they would tell me what they wanted to be when they grow up, most of them wanted to be Boda drivers like someone in their family.

I went back to Uganda years later with a group of friends, and we were sitting around with a TV on in the common room, when suddenly a friend yelled out "Oh my God, you're on TV." They had been replaying the same episode for over 5 years due to the novelty of having a Mzungu on the show!!

I really struggled when I had to leave Uganda. My time was coming to an end there, I'd already booked my flights, which were not able to be changed. In my time I had developed a deep bond with a particular little boy named William (my dad's name). His Ugandan name was Tumisimi, meaning 'the gift'. I wanted to bundle him up and take him with me, to give him all the love he needed, but unfortunately it wouldn't have been a suitable thing to do as a young, single woman on the road.

As fate would have it, it was nap time when my car came to pick me up. I just remember going over to him and saying a little prayer that someone would take him, and he'd be adopted to an amazing family. I gave him a kiss on the cheek and walked out to the car with tears streaming down my face. I had maybe put more emphasis on this connection due to the name he shared with my father, but in some way

I felt it was a message that I would be able to feel connections again that would fill the void I had felt since losing my dad. That little boy had made more impact to my life than he will ever know.

From Uganda, I headed back to London and caught up with one of my best friends from the stripping scene in Perth. Heidi had been there through my dad's death, we had travelled and worked together and we had partied hard. It had been a few years since I had last seen her and I was nervous to see how our relationship would be. I arrived at her nearest train station, we went back to hers and I quickly realised I had nothing to be nervous about! We were getting ready to go out and hit the town that night and she was on the toilet as I was in the shower, leg up, shaving my cha cha. I have always thought that the test of a true friendship is the ability to be naked and take a piss in front of one another…I think it's my gauge for how comfortable we can feel with each other.

That night we headed out on a bender full of booze and cocaine. London brought up a lot of emotion for me. The consumerism, the waste, the lack of appreciation for people's lives that I just couldn't watch – it made me furious. I didn't know how to reconcile where I had been, and the lessons that I'd learned, and integrate them into where I was. I found it really difficult to be able to have conversations with people on a "lower" level, and I guess it created a little bit of an isolation. Conversations about the weather and material objects seemed infantile. I wanted to shake people…didn't they know what was going on in the rest of the world?? I began to self-medicate again to "conform" to this idea of normality and force myself to stop thinking about poor William and all the babies I'd left behind.

Forever the party girl and pretty good at this point at avoiding my true feelings, I took off from London, bound for Prague. With the European summer now well underway it was a beautiful place for me to try to shake off this feeling of needing something deeper in my existence. I traveled with two of the coolest dudes I've ever met, Johnny and Marco. I had met Johnny when he had couch surfed the year prior at my place in Cronulla. We traveled through Prague, Germany, Paris and Amsterdam together. The whole trip was full of running for trains, missing trains, hunting for cheap places to stay, eat and drink. I began experiencing that feeling of awe again. One life-altering experience was taking magic mushrooms in in Amsterdam.

I began with a very small, low dose so I could ease into the trip, but boys being boys they downed an entire packet. From what we had been told they could take anywhere up to six hours to come on, so when they hit with full impact within half an hour we were really flying. Our hostel was next to a massive park in the centre of the city. We were far too paranoid to stay in the hostel so we made out way to the park just as the sun was setting. My body felt soft and fuzzy, I had never felt like this before, out of this world. As we all lay on the grass the leaves on the trees began twirling and vining down towards my face and my body felt that it was becoming one with the grass. I could finally feel the aliveness and connection with nature I had heard about before. In that moment I also made the connection to mushroom use and the story of Alice In Wonderland. I'm not pro-hallucinogenic but for me it was a really empowering experience. In the right doses, company and situation it can be truly magical and mind-expanding. I don't want anyone reading this to feel like I'm condoning drug use by any means, but it's part of my story, one of the things that has shaped me.

I bid the guys farewell in Paris. After a few solid weeks on the road they had become like family. It was bittersweet as I had Heidi to meet for La Tomatina (the tomato fight) in Spain, but I had developed quite an attraction with Johnny. We had become lovers from very early on in our travels – our souls were drawn to one another, the sex was amazing, we couldn't get enough of eachother. He had just lost his father before taking his trip and we were a great comfort to one another. But I had to honour my word, having made the promise not to get entangled in another relationship for at least a year, so off to Spain I went, and with a 17-hour train ride ahead I settled in for the long haul.

Arriving in Spain to Heidi and her boyfriend was awkward. He had decided he was coming only a short time earlier. He really didn't like me, because I could see how awfully he treated her, and I very bluntly let her know that she deserved a lot better. After the tomato fight, **how many** nights in Valencia we ended up making it across to Ibiza. We had a few nights out at the club and more often than not someone having an after party in their room. Heidi and Jack had left the club early one night – I had assumed it was to go have rockstar sex and so a few hours later decided it would be okay to bring the party back to ours. Heidi answered the door, bawling her eyes out, black mascara staining her cheeks. She'd finally mustered up the courage to leave him – she was afraid that going back to the UK with him in a few days may weaken her resolve on the break up. I was about to take off to Greece in a few days and made an offer she couldn't resist.

All the way to the airport I remember thinking, "She may chicken out. She may turn around and leave." But this was the next impromptu part of the trip.

"Look, I've got cash, you can pay me back later," I told her.

"I've got a credit card," she said. "And I'm happy to pay that back later." We partied our way through Athens, Santorini and Mykonos. We really developed a feeling of trust on this part of our trip. Very limited places had Amex access and my card was swallowed. People bought us food, helped us get ferry tickets and organise new cards.

I was beginning to hit a wall with all the partying, and my soul was screaming now louder than ever. I kept getting this deep calling to head to an ashram I had heard about in Pune, India. I had no further details, but had managed to convince Heidi to come for the journey. So, with no idea what to expect, we booked our flights at an internet café (without reading the fine print). We made the journey back to the mainland and out of the city, and managed to get all the way out to the airport on the back of a massive hangover. We stood there waiting with our tickets, faces brimming with all the wonder and adventure of what was yet to come.

We stepped up to the check in counter and were asked, "Where are your visa's girls?"

"Oh, no, we're Australian," I replied. "We don't need Visa's."

"It's India," she laughed. "Everybody needs Visas." After much back and forth we proceeded to lose 880 euros between us. By then, it was too late to catch a train back to the city, so we asked, "Where is the next flight to?" She said it was to Kathmandu in Nepal, and we looked at each other thinking, "fuck it!" What's a little detour on the road, so to speak. My ignorance and lack of geographical knowledge led us to believe we were in Tibet for the first week or so!!

Luckily, we had Heidi's dad's Amex card for the flights (we paid them back but it was a good stop gap). Heidi was faced with a hell of a lot to process – not only was she coming to terms with her breakup, but as she only now revealed, she had never been to any kind of third world country. Seeing the poverty and way of life in these places can definitely be a huge challenge. Looking back now, again, we should have maybe done a little bit of research into where we were going. There was actually a government coup on at the time – there were lock-ins, shutdowns and curfews.

We spent some time in the hustle and bustle of Kathmandu, finding our favourite Indian-inspired meals. I was eating Paneer Butter Masala as well as this buffalo and dumpling soup like it was going out of fashion. We'd been to some nightclubs that were actually open illegally, so when we went it was like a lock-in. Our naivety probably wouldn't have helped us from getting in a whole lot of trouble if we had been in the club as it was raided by local police. Eventually, we got on to the business of actualising what we had planned to do from the start, which was to dry out and find some peace and some zen. We checked ourselves into an Osho Tapoban in the deep jungle of Nepal, again diving in head first with little research or knowledge of what to expect. There were no other Westerners there, and I guess to some it could have appeared like a cult, but it was exactly what we needed at the time. We expected to go there and do some kind of regular omming, chanting and seated meditations in our quest become one with the universe.

We were in for a rude awakening as we switched our hippy pants and t-shirts for long maroon robes. We left our travelling hippy persona at the door, all set to find our zen. We were guided to the main hall where we found a room of 150 people all in matching maroon robes, shaking and wobbling and moving around like crazy people. I felt so embarrassed and uncomfortable for them and thought, "there is no fucking way I will be caught dead doing that!"

"What the fuck have we got ourselves into?" We whispered to each other and after a short discussion came to the consensus if you cant beat em, join em! So there I was, every inch of my body feeling self-conscious and mortified – this was an Osho active or dynamic meditation. I had never moved like this in front of a room of people without a few drinks under my belt. We began shaking our hands and slowly allowing the shaking to take over our bodies. This was, essentially, to move whatever is in the nervous system at the time out of the body, to kind of shake any excess energy out. I don't know if that's scientifically what it's for, but that's what it felt like to me.

> "My meditation is simple. It does not require any complex practices. It is simple. It is singing. It is dancing. It is sitting silently."
>
> — **Osho**

Then I'm pretty sure we began jumping, jumping like you would imagine a Maasai warrior in Kenya when they're jumping, holding the sticks. An entire room of people jumping in unison. The next 15 minutes was for expressing whatever had moved in your body previously, so if you felt like laughing like a hyena or giggling or screaming or crying, you were given full permission to do so. On the first day, my voice was very quiet. I was very stifled. I'd never been "given" this much freedom to just express what was running through my veins! By day two I was screaming from the rooftops into the jungle. I had never felt so free.

Next came the silent, sit still style meditation we were prepared for. Usually I would dread this as I struggled with my thoughts, as well as with fidgeting etc, but this time it was the easiest 15-minute meditation I've ever done. I was completely still and completely thoughtless – well as thoughtless as I could be at the time. I could have sat there for hours. This form of meditation made complete sense. We spent the next few days attending 3-5 meditation or movement classes per day.

From the Tapoban we moved to a yoga school at the foot of the Himalayas in the town of Pokhara. We did some cleansing, chanting, yoga. Things were a little less serious here than at the previous ashram, but there was a definite routine, something which we had desperately needed after six weeks on the road together. Our time was coming to an end – Heidi knew it was time to head back to the big smoke of London and face moving on with her new life. I actually had no idea what I was going to be doing, until one night in a discussion over a cup of chai I mentioned, "I've heard that Dubai's really good for money. Maybe I could go and personal train over there."

The next day, I went into the old school internet cafés and logged into my email, and something caught my eye in the headlines. It said, 'VIP hostesses needed for club in Dubai.' Now, this was from an agency that I'd only ever worked for once before, years earlier, and I had actually never even met them in person. They had hired me from my pictures for a job in Sydney. Of course, the synchronicity of me mentioning Dubai the night before and this email made me reply posthaste. Another meant to be moment? We corresponded on the contract to and fro for a few weeks, finally agreeing that a month later I would be moving out to Dubai to be part of a team to help promote and upsell alcohol at a very affluent bar.

> "In mathematics, two angles that are said to coincide fit together perfectly. The word "coincidence" does not describe luck or mistakes. It describes that which fits together perfectly."
> **- Wayne Dyer**

I became part of a team of eight girls selected from New Zealand and Australia. So again, with no knowledge about the culture, I signed my life away, deciding that it was time for the next adventure. I guess at the time, I had an idea in my head that I would go for six months, replenish my bank account and head back on the open road. Boy was I wrong! What is it they say? "If you want to make God laugh, tell him your plans," because my life turned out very, very differently, but I'm saving that for the next chapter!

CHAPTER SIX
DO YOU NEED A VISA?

So here I am, signing my life away on the dotted line, all the t's and i's crossed and dotted. What does any 24-year-old girl do to make sure that she's made the right decision? Book in and see a fortune teller, of course. My mum found a great psychic in Perth and booked the both of us in. I had always been somewhat of a believer – I believe readers will help you to affirm whether you are on the right path either way. The trouble can be when you start to mould your life to fit what you have been told! I needed a confirmation from the universe that I was headed in the right direction. Dubai!!! Holy shit, what had I just agreed to? But my other alternative was heading back to Sydney, and it just didn't feel like I was done with exploring yet.

I was back in Perth spending some time with my sister and my beautiful new nephew, Isaiah. My sister and I, although it wasn't strained, had a bit of a distant relationship. I had moved out at 16, when she was 13, and so I didn't really get to know her as a human until much later in life, at least in terms of what she stood for, what she enjoyed, and what her values were. Until she became a mother I had just seen her as my annoying little sis. It took me a while to wrap my head around the fact that she was now a Mama! After the emotional journey of childbirth and becoming a mother my sister shared with me that when I had moved out she had felt a little abandoned and left behind. I guess it was a reflection of the selfish side of me that had got out and never wanted to look back. Now that she had a family of her own I wanted things to be different and I am so glad we got the opportunity to be able spend some time bonding over her new bubba!

As long as I can remember I have had this strange ability to block out wherever I was last and just be with the people I was with in that moment. I still don't know if it's that I am being present or that I have had to learn to compartmentalise my life to make leaving places easier. Either way, as a result I have hurt my fair share of people along the way. It is something I am so conscious not to do now.

Anyway, back to the psychic. I sit down and she starts talking about how in six weeks there's going to be really good news and how there's going to be a man in uniform, with a link to America.

"Lots of people will look up to him and he will have lots of friends and be well liked in his friends circle." My immediate reaction was to say, "Ew. I don't like American men." No offense to anybody out there who is American, but there was something about the accent that grated on me. So I took it all on board with a giant pinch of salt but felt assured by what else she had said – that this move would be a great step in the right direction and that I should definitely go ahead, that this would trigger a domino effect of things that were ready to come to me.

Later that day I was chatting with my sister and I remember so clearly her saying to me, "You're almost 25, do you really think you should be off gallivanting around the world? Don't you think you should be finding a nice man to settle down with?" That moment planted a seed in my mind that I was behind the eight ball. What was I doing with my life? I didn't feel ready but it seemed the next chronological step for someone my age. In the suburbs of Perth at the time, most of my friendship group had children, were engaged, married or pregnant.

I'd enjoyed the year of just finding out who I was without a man. I'd acquired some new tools and thought that I'd healed my entire life by attending a couple of shaking meditation sessions and a yoga ashram. Little did I know, this was just the first couple of layers of the onion and there were many more to go. I had merely scratched the surface.

I began to question myself. What was I doing? I should probably have at least a steady partner by now! What was wrong with me? With my sister's ideals lodged in my brain, I boarded the plane and set off for my new life in Dubai. I landed in the wee hours of the morning and was picked up by one of the managers and taken to my new apartment.

The apartment had two bedrooms and was to be shared between four girls. There had already been another four girls that had been flown over earlier, so I was expecting them to be in my building and thought that at least somebody else would be there. When I got dropped off in this beautiful building, just near the Dubai mall (which was still being built) I felt like I was in a ghost town, and after the manager left, I started to panic.

I was in this building, in a foreign country, having not read much into my contract, left to my own devices, no internet or mobile phone in your hand back then, thinking, "What the fuck have I done?" The amount of times I've said this sentence to myself in my life is …in my life is…well I would be a billionaire if I had a dollar for every time. As I was wondering it once again, I all of a sudden thought, "Holy shit. Maybe I've just got myself sold into some kind of sex trafficking ring and they're going to bring other girls and we're just going to be tied to this bed in chains."

Something that I can credit my mother with is picking up her anxious, catastrophising tendencies. I always go to the worst, worst thing, and my brain decides that's definitely what's going to happen. My body was almost frozen with fear, I went into a complete freeze, trying to regulate my breathing and talk myself out of it. Eventually I must've dozed off to sleep, and in the light of day, I no longer felt the same panic.

During the next day, three other girls arrived and I instantly had a new family. When we had all arrived, we were taken to a group place together, and spent the next four weeks training, learning about etiquette, promotion, and fine-tuning our look. Dubai is a very aesthetically-focused place, and they expected us to be in the gym every day, to have blonde hair, and to have perfect nails, and they gave us an allowance to do so.

In the back end of the club there had been holdups with building permits, licenses and all those kinds of things, so we were literally being paid to party. Eight twenty-something-year-old girls, given a salary, no work for now and a shitload of free time! There were so many clubs and parties in Dubai I was actually blown away. There went my idea of living a clean, healthy lifestyle and saving to get back on the road!

It was like we were superstars, the new girls in town. We were taken in limos to parties, to home nightclubs, boat parties, helicopter rides – a whirlwind of extreme lavishness. There's a part of me that went along with it and enjoyed this new starry-eyed life, being treated like a VIP, but the hangovers and the partying were starting to take their toll on me emotionally. I was desperately searching for a way out because I knew that if I didn't watch myself I could get lost in it.

Looking back, I realise that was my way of coping without really addressing the fact that, "Hey, I've just relocated countries, just been in Africa and left my life as I know it." I had seen and experienced a lot. When I don't feel grounded, safe and settled, I subconsciously turn to booze to avoid all the fears that arise with now being totally "alone". I was also 25 and it's what all the other girls were doing, so it was hard for me to have my boundaries and say, "No, I'm staying in," Even when that's what my soul was craving.

The girls were amazing and they totally became my new family, and to this day we keep in touch. Like any group of people together, there were personality clashes, but for the most part I think we got through it fairly unscathed. Finally it came to opening night at the nightclub, which was called Bang, it was a disaster and a success all in one. We hadn't had a soft run yet, so it was basically just chaos that we covered over with smiles and laughter.

Our job was to man each table, serve the drinks, up-sell and entice people to buy bigger, better bottles of champagne than the table next to them. In the process they would spend ridiculous amounts of money – basically proving whose cock was the biggest. Dubai is super well-known for its lavish partying. To begin with, I judged them a lot for being out partying. I thought, "How can you be Muslim and be saying one thing and then doing another?" I experienced a fair bit of hypocrisy, but I still played into the judgment until I realised there was no other option. When you're born as an Emirati in Dubai, you, by default, become a Muslim. I guess these young men, mainly, were out there partying and just doing what every other kid had been doing at that age, so could I really hold that against them? The experience really taught me to have a little bit more compassion and understanding for others. Yes they were Muslim but that didn't define people in their entirety. It was just one facet of their identity, much like me with stripping – something I did but not an all-encompassing aspect of my personality.

One of these party nights when I'd been out and about, it was heading towards Christmas Day, and it was bringing up a lot for me. I had been in contact with my ex who I had moved to Sydney with, Owen. When I had been back in Perth, we'd rekindled things and became lovers for the month that I was there. I really wanted more, I wanted him to fight and tell me to stay and tell me that he wanted me and that I was the one. I struggled to let go of it.

I remember that Christmas Day, talking to him and bawling my eyes out about feeling lonely, isolated and drowning in this new party environment. I was hungover as hell, with a new friendship group, and one of the ladies in the house had been invited to an "Orphans" Christmas (for those living away from family during the festive cheer). These weren't the typical kind of Emirati people that we had been seeing in the clubs, this was a bunch of misfits – expat brats, you would say. They were brought up in the land of the sand, the cool kids, most of them quite well off with parents who had been there for years, and some of them semi-entitled types.

The invite said the more the merrier so, nursing a hangover from hell, I thought the only thing I could do was to drink through this. It sure beat the idea of being in the apartment on my own. I started drinking again and getting into the spirit of things. The place was huge, an older style Arabic villa. I wandered around, having a sticky beak, finding out where the food, drinks and toilets were, before finding myself a place to perch. I had a vodka and cranberry in hand as I wandered over toward where some of my flatmates were sitting.

There must've been about 60 people at this party. On the way over to my flatmates I walked through a group of people and a guys voice yells out, "Oi, marry me." Being known for my quick wit and banter, I replied, "Why? Do you need a visa?" He said, "Yes." Something clicked in me, that spontaneous part of me, and I said, "Okay, I can get you a visa if you marry me. I've a job here." Little did I know that he didn't need one, he already had his own visa, but it started us having a conversation.

The rest of the night became quite blurry. I don't really recall what happened, but when it was recounted back to me what had occurred, I found out that one of my friends had married us that night, jokingly, in the kitchen. I was wearing a Red Bull ring pull on my finger and he was wearing my big maroon and gold flower ring, which were all the rage at the time – those big, huge tacky rings from Accessorize or something.

The party ended and we ended up rolling back to his hotel room, where he had been staying because he was living an hour and a half away. Myself, my girlfriend, Mel, and this guy Boston. He did the gentlemanly thing and let us pass out on his double bed whilst he slept on the couch. When we awoke the next morning the fear that went through me of: where am I? Who am I? What happened? It was like a scene from, "Dude, where's my car?" When I strung back together what had happened the night before, I started to panic about where he was because when we awoke he wasn't on the couch.

I checked my phone and saw that Boston had texted me to say that he couldn't wake us and had gone for a surf. My girlfriend and I ordered food to the bed and decided that we were so hungover that the only thing we could do was pull ourselves together and go out on another escapade. This time we headed to Irish Village and partied there, after a few drinks and some more Dutch courage I messaged Boston asking what he was up to. My body at this stage was screaming at me, my skin was awful, I felt bloated as all fuck, but I continued on! We headed to a place called 360, an outdoor bar surrounded by ocean – it was beautiful.

There was just something about this guy. He was cheeky, funny, had an amazing tan, turquoise blue eyes, and felt really familiar to me. I wanted to be around him, and I had this fear at the same time, a feeling that I had a clock ticking against me. I was 25 and I thought I better find some way to settle down. I was missing Owen, feeling isolated and lonely, so a year to the day after my "man ban" started, I said to myself, "All right, I'm ready for a new relationship." I had also remembered what the psychic said about meeting a man in uniform (this new guy was training to become a pilot) with an American connection – he was Australian but his name was Boston! So I made a beeline for him!

We went all in. We were in from the get-go. A week after I met Boston I said to him, "Look, don't play games with me. If I text you, respond. Don't play the waiting game." At the time, I knew very little about the psychology of men and women in relationships – in retrospect, I completely emasculated him from the get go and became the driving force behind our relationship. I did what I had seen in the majority of relationships around me.

There was a little bit of pressure for him to figure himself out too. He thought that he would find his happiness in somebody else as well, so with very little knowledge about each other, we thought, "Fuck it. Let's get married." I felt like I had tried it the old fashioned way, tried dating, living together and doing all those things that made it feel a little safer at first. Why not give this a go, you know? You only live once. I felt like I had asked all the right questions to try to avoid the patterns that had played out in my past relationships.

I asked what his away roster would be like, since he was training to become a pilot. He said, "No, problems. I only do short hauls, there and back, so I'll be home at night." I was happy with that. His family was still together and appeared to be functioning. He'd had a nice upbringing, gone to a nice school, had amazing job prospects. He checked a lot of boxes on the list for husband material.

All of those things looked great on paper, but on the deeper side of things, I didn't ask the important questions: am I compatible with this man? What are his opinions on life? What does he feel about certain world issues? It was only years later that I found these things out. Two months in I asked, "Were you serious about what you said when I walked past you? 'Oi, marry me.'" And he said, "Yes."

That was it. At the end of February my mum came out on holidays with my Aunty Jen and we decided that we were going to announce our engagement. So two months after meeting each other it was decided that we were to be married by the end of August that year. We spent the next few months working on our future plans, instead of spending it really getting to know each other.

This became our thing. We found commonality in reaching for goals, planning trips, saving for cars and things like that. Our relationship didn't ever flourish by sitting and talking to each other. It was heavily based on setting goals and reaching those together, but we really didn't have much of an idea who the other was at heart.

In the lead up to the wedding I starting to get a little bit of cold feet, and I thought that this may have been my commitment issues. I began noticing that we didn't talk much at all, that he would rarely initiate conversation with me, and the sex had slowed dramatically. I convinced myself that I was self-sabotaging, rather than purely observing that we may not have been a match. I kept pushing it away and pushing it down, hoping things would change. He became very serious, not like the fun loving guy I had met months prior.

Although it wasn't all bad – we rarely fought – I just felt this loneliness even whilst sitting right next to him. It felt all we had was this promise to each other, and when I commit to something, I work and I work to make it happen. Rather, I sometimes flog a dead horse!

There was a part of my ego that really didn't want to let go of this marriage. We were organising this beautiful fairytale wedding and I liked the story that it came with. I walked past him and he said, "Oi, marry me," so we were getting married. That's the Disney shit that we think we all need in life, that has been pummeled down our throats since we were three years old. This one's going to be the one, and somehow I would be a failure if I couldn't make it work.

On the outside, on Facebook, to everybody else, to him, I put on my smiley face. I would pretend that I was in this happy bubble. But his moods dropped and he pulled away further. I felt like I had become his cheerleader and totally let go of what I wanted to do in life, and instead was focused only on making him happy. I became a martyr, and totally let go of the idea that I was entitled to have sex in my relationship, or that I was entitled to long for conversation. I felt that I was being shallow by desiring those things. In hindsight, I realise now that it wasn't selfless and it wasn't in the name of love. It was a way of denying myself what we're innately here to be – joyful, connected and close. Oh, how I ached for it.

Back to the club! A few months after opening, it got shut down by the powers that be. It had been a beautiful place, the bar was completely made of Swarovski crystal, it was decadent in every sense of the word. It was such a shame but at the same time I had been struggling with insomnia hugely and, since it was still legal to smoke inside, I had found myself constantly coughing and spluttering. This was just before the wedding so I moved in with Boston to this very small country town called Al Ain. There weren't very many westerners out there and even fewer western women. Boston was training all day every day, I didn't have a job at this point, and aside from doing bits and pieces of personal training for some Emirati women – which I really enjoyed – for the most part I sat in the bedroom of a sharehouse watching Playboy Mansion box sets.

I fell into a really deep depression and couldn't be motivated to get out of my bed or do anything. I think it was this realisation that I had kind of signed my life away and not really taken into account how it would affect me. Most of my friends from Dubai had to leave when the job fell through and the only person that I had, aside from one beautiful friend who I'm still close with now, was this half-stranger soon-to-be-husband in a relationship that wasn't fulfilling any of my needs.

Both too proud to quit and walk away, we played house for a few years. There were some fun times for sure. We traveled a lot. I just never felt really connected to him in the way that I would have liked to with a lover, partner or a husband. This played out and we became more distant until it was like sitting on the couch with a complete stranger. He'd be on his phone or watching TV, and I'd be typing and trying to find myself a way to make money over there.

There was a lot of strain and tension in the relationship. I would quite often fly between Perth and Dubai just to try to get that social aspect and be around friends and family for support, because aside from doing odds and ends of modeling and hair and makeup, I was pretty much on my own during the bulk of the days, sitting and waiting for him to come home. My life really did centre around whatever he was doing and wherever he would be.

I was lucky enough in the UAE to meet and party with the likes of Simon Pegg and Jeremy Renner, and have group dinners with Oliver Stone and Maroon 5. I was flown to Pakistan, Bahrain, Oman, Qatar and Kuwait on modeling assignments. I met the King of Bahrain and advised the Abu Dhabi Royal Family on nutrition. I went to the Sheikas (the female royals) Palace and assisted in the running of a boot camp. The grounds were spectacular, truly amazing. There were gazelles roaming free, white owls flying around and I got lost trying to find the bathroom!

It was very impressive. Despite the fact that I was living the high life, however, I couldn't shake the empty feeling.

When he would get home, Boston was tired from flying because no matter how hard I had tried to vet the fact that he wouldn't be away, it didn't quite work out that way. Very shortly after he started flying he applied to go onto a bigger airplane which meant he was flying quite a bit and doing longer hauls. I was a lady in waiting, just waiting for him to come home, waiting for him to want to do something, waiting for him to get holidays so we could go and enjoy the cheap travel.

Without too much purpose in my life, I began to really sink and doubt all the choices that I had made. For me, I felt the only thing that I could do was work on myself, and that became my new purpose. The more I worked on myself, the more I realised that I maybe wasn't in my truest alignment, but hindsight is 20/20 vision. At the time, I was just trying to fix myself and somehow fix my relationship by being more present. I thought by working tirelessly on my own acceptance and compassion I could begin to feel fulfilled with what was. I believed if I wished for it hard enough we could turn things around.

Despite the difficulties, I'm very grateful for and humbled by the experience. It almost feels like it was another lifetime ago now. It's interesting how life segments itself, and I am definitely not the same person that I was then. I've experienced so much growth and evolution. The next part of my life was to be one of the biggest ongoing evolutions yet – becoming a mother…

CHAPTER SEVEN

MY SHINING LIGHT

Boston and I were always such a goal-oriented couple. We ticked off moving in, we ticked off engagement parties, we ticked off getting married, we ticked off traveling together, and so it felt like the natural progression was to talk about children. The common goal gave us something to talk about and covered our deep incompatibility. I just remember wishing that he could fuck my mind as well as my body. By now neither of the two things were happening often at all. I was yearning for passion, not just physically but mentally. I love to chat about feelings, the psyche, the mysteries of the universe and such, and the more I was learning the more I was realising we weren't on the same page. Boston unknowingly chased his future happiness. He would be happy when he reached the next step, and our next future happy, subconsciously, was parenting.

Very early on in our relationship I had brought up that ideally I would love to adopt in the future. Boston had agreed at the time but I wanted to really be sure that he was agreeing not just to please me, but because he saw why or how it could be a positive thing, like assisting the greater good in some kind of way. It was our small piece to try to give back.

I organised a trip to Uganda – this time it was just a quick 10-day-er – and we actually had a lot of fun. We went with another couple. I had a friend down there running her own very ethically-organised foundation, so we went in and we visited and we saw everyone there and Boston got the opportunity to connect with my WHY! That was a really important piece of the journey for me.

Aside from the orphanages, we went and trekked into the Bwindi Impenetrable Forest, which as the name suggests is quite a task. There's knee-deep foliage, thorns on every tree branch, and you're wading through leeches, rain and all kinds of things for the chance to be lucky enough to sight gorillas in the wild. Luckily for us, and especially me, who was – surprise, surprise – totally unprepared for said Impenetrable Forest, we had only been walking for about 45 minutes when we stumbled upon a massive Silverback. This guy would've been about 27, with incisors the size of elephant tusks it seemed. He was very warily watching us out of the periphery of his vision. He was at the bottom of a bank of a hill, and we had somehow gotten trapped in this little pocket above him. There was also what I guessed was a young mother and a little baby playing around and actually being quite social, acting up for the cameras.

We were busy watching the mum and baby interact with us and each other when, next minute, we were faced with a 250-kilo gorilla charging up the hill directly towards us. Just as we were trying to scramble back higher up the hill and get away from this guy, he swept the mum and the baby out of the way with a brisk flick of his hand and turned around and sat down, crossing his arms as if to say, "this is my space," fully owning it. I must say my heart was in my mouth. I was panicking. I have never seen people scramble so quickly in their lives. Now, we were with guards should anything have gone wrong, but that would have also involved harming the animals and that wasn't the reason we were there. We were there to observe them in their natural habitat.

Funnily enough, this big guy just sat down and he kept staring, baring his teeth and giving us a look which said, "I can fucking see you. Watch it." It was like this little warning, but he didn't need to prove or assert himself with any other kind of behavior. We just knew to tread very carefully. The guide told us that, he just wanted to be out of the rain and in this spot, the trees were providing a canopy-like shelter for him.

It was a fascinating experience and one that I will never, ever forget. Gorillas aside, we also learned a lot about the Ugandan people living in those areas. The delicacy there isn't fried chips. It's fried crickets. I couldn't at that time bring myself to have one. I was already feeling a bit car sick from going around and around and up and down the mountains to get to the trek.

By the end of this trip and both Boston and I had cemented the idea that he was open and understood my why behind wanting to adopt, so when we got back we started gung ho into the process. I can't remember what year this was. I'm not too sure, sometimes it all hazes together, but we started chipping away at all the paperwork, documentation and red tape that we had to go through just to start the process. Neither of us was in any kind of rush, but it gave us a common goal, it gave us a thing that we were working towards, it gave us a point of communication, and so we started the process.

We went through the counseling where they check your mental stability, how you are as a couple and ask you about your own parents and childhood. Piece by piece you put together a dossier and build this case that proves that you're good people. Deep down, we are good people. During the process of getting this dossier already, I remember sitting bolt upright in the middle of the night, when we had been plugging along, and saying, "Boston, we need to go now. We need to do this adoption now." Something had possessed me. It was like an internal knowing. I had the same feeling about selling my house. I had the same feeling about going on a trip. It was almost like it wasn't me. I wasn't the one pushing this thing. Something was coming through me and driving me.

I became like a mad woman and within a month we'd finalised and finished everything. I had flown down the day afterwards straight to Ethiopia. We had looked at Uganda as an option, but we couldn't confirm that we would definitely get Australian citizenship on the other end, and we couldn't risk having a child that was stuck in no man's land because that wouldn't be fair on anybody. We knew some couples that had gone through Ethiopia. They knew the process and we didn't need to reinvent the wheel. We just wanted to follow verbatim what they did and make it as easy as possible for ourselves.

I flew down on May 25th, 2012. There was another couple that I had been speaking to online who I knew were flying down at the same time, and they weren't hard to spot at the airport with their hands full of bags of nappies to take to the orphanage, so I went over at the gate and introduced myself. That became our little family for this process. It was almost strange that Boston wasn't there during the adoption process, and the knowledge that this was going to be a journey to motherhood that I'd do, for the most part, alone.

Michael and Stella and I trundled off to the jungle, so to speak, and landed in Ethiopia. We went to a few orphanages, handing in our dossiers without much luck. We were told that it could be a few months or closer to the end of the year until there were any children that became available in the city. Although apprehensive and excited for this journey, none of us were in a huge rush either. We all had this feeling of being on the edge of something huge and life-changing, yet like an open-ended ticket, with no real idea of when it would happen.

The next day I was supposed to be flying back to Dubai after I'd done my initial interviews with a few places. I had really only applied at one orphanage after doing background checks and making sure that they were as kosher, legitimate and as transparent as possible with the adoptions – that it was definitely a child that needed a home and didn't have known existing family. In our dossier we said a boy or girl between zero and one years old, but that we would prefer a younger girl. I didn't want it to be like a shopping catalogue or a cart on Amazon where you clicked what you wanted and it got delivered to you. I just trusted that the universe would send whoever needed us and whomever we needed.

Just as I was getting ready to head back to Dubai I got a phone call, asking if I could come back in to the one of the orphanages. It was the Missionaries of Charity, which was a Mother Teresa-based orphanage, and they had also called back Michael and Stella. We all went into the room and got interviewed by the Head Sister there. She sat down and said that two babies had actually just become available. Their prospective parents had applied at multiple places and been matched elsewhere.

"There's a boy and a girl. Who wants what?" In the shock, I was thinking that we couldn't decide that. That's not for us to say. We'd just met on the plane, how could we decide this for each other? Fortunately, Sister took the ball out of our court by simply pointing to me and saying, "You have the girl."

I was almost nervous to ask the next question. The idea of meeting this human who is already alive and already somehow connected to me was just overwhelming. I squeaked out, "Are they here? Can we meet them?"

"Yes, they're upstairs," Sister replied. "We're just going to get them changed and bring them down."

That was the most life-changing moment of my entire life. I was expecting to put my dossier in and not hear anything for a year or so, and the next day I was holding my baby in my arms. I knew the minute I held her, when she was holding her fists up next to her face like she was really aware and she was ready to take on the world, "That's my girl." Her middle name is Love as it's the only thing that I could feel in that moment. I have a feeling we have done this thing called life before – maybe she was a grandmother figure to me in the past. It quite often comes out in our mother/daughter relationship where I feel that, somehow, she's the wise one teaching me.

Needless to say, I was stunned, emotional, joyful and petrified all at once. Later that day, we had to take them out to get an HIV test to make sure that they didn't test positive because on the other end we wouldn't be able to adopt them due to the visa issues it would create for the Middle East. So we'd already met these children, fallen in love with them, and then we had to wait to find out whether we were actually allowed to take them with us.

We took them to the hospital and had to get them their first little needle extractions. Yeah, it was there that we realised what being a parent was going to be, and again, it was something I'd thrown myself into completely unprepared. I was messaging Boston and trying to send photos through to him of our new precious package, but the wifi was awful and it took hours to get them to him. By the time they got through he was out with some mates and he was ecstatic. Already this little girl was bringing people together.

I headed back to Dubai the next day because I couldn't afford to stay down in Ethiopia until the court process, and it was the toughest two weeks of my life. We were still awaiting the results of the HIV test, and Stella and I spoke regularly, hypothesising about all the possible scenarios and outcomes. I felt this duty of care to her regardless of what the test came back as. Luckily for us they came back with the negative or positive, whichever one it is, result that means that she was free from HIV.

The only information we had on her was that she was from the northern town of Gonder and that she had been found by a policewoman behind the hospital when she was an estimated ten days old. She had spent the next month in an orphanage in Gonder and when there were enough children to "fill the truck" they drove the babies down to the capital. Initially we were appalled to hear of their journey down, but looking back I can see the logic in it. The babies, including Michael and Stella's new son, were wrapped in blankets and placed in fruit boxes. The boxes were packed in tightly next to each other to stop them from jiggling around too much on the bumpy 12 hour ride to

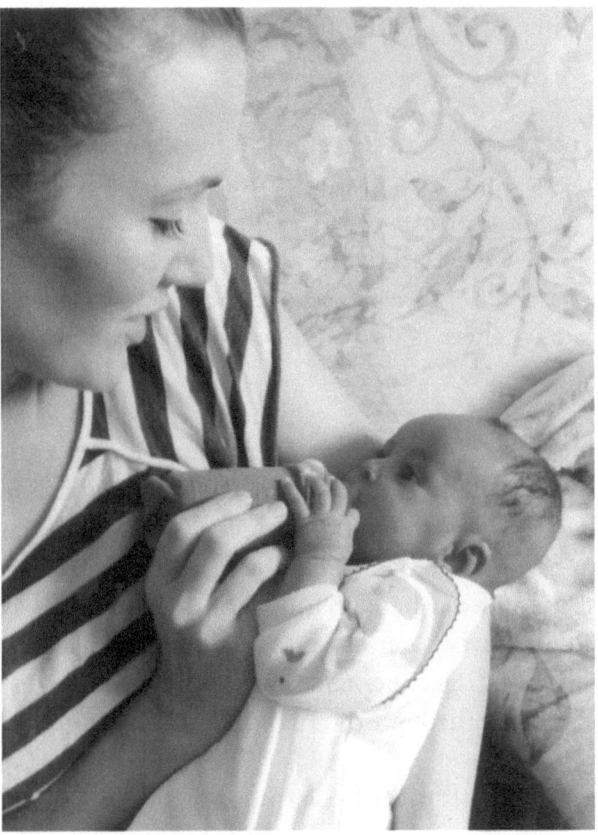

the city. There was a driver and a nurse to feed and change the babies during their journey.

The next waiting game was for our court dates. We had six weeks to try to squeeze our hearing in, otherwise we would have to wait until nearer to the end of the year when the courts reopened. It's not an ideal situation to have your baby sitting in an orphanage when they could be at home bonding with you. Again, the luck of the Irish was on our side and we got a court date for July 16 or 17. So there we were, July 2012, once again with only Michael, Stella and I present. Boston was saving his time off for when we actually got the baby back home. Fortunately everything went smoothly, and after a few requests for paperwork and a short hearing, we all became parents!!! We got the babies from the orphanage the next day.

We were kind of the blind leading the blind, realising that we had no idea what to do. It was like a production line of trying to figure out how to mix up formula bottles, how to bath and how to change their nappies. We were all in the room together helping each other out. I was extremely grateful to have met such an awesome couple on the journey – there is no way I could have ever imagined doing this alone.

The next week or so was spent getting passports and finalising paperwork, until finally, it was time to bring them back home to the UAE. We were so lucky that our daughter slept through the night. She was a fairly easy, passive baby. She talked a lot, chatted and engaged and I "wore" her a lot. I had a handful of different baby carriers and absolutely loved having her close to my chest as I felt like it really quickened our bonding experience. We felt very blessed as she was an easy baby that slept through the night from the get go.

On the other hand, after the honeymoon period of having her home and the process of her settling in, there was more and more of a disconnect from my husband. I felt him pulling away more and more. I'd constantly bring this up with him, but I think by this stage the damage had already been done. I began to feel isolated during the transition to motherhood – we were living in a compound in Abu Dhabi at the time, I'd put her to bed at five o'clock, and although I had one very close friend I was missing the support of my family and friends. Not having a close relationship with my husband was really starting to eat away at me. I started to feel like I was a square peg in a round hole, like I was having to contain myself and dull down parts of myself to fit into what his ideal of a woman was.

At a time that I thought should be the most enjoyable in my life, I began self-medicating – highly functioning, but very dependent on wine to soften the blow. This had begun in the months after Love had come to join our new family. I quite often found myself alone with Boston away flying, and I found solace in my wine glass. Love slept through the night from the get go so I had many hours to fill whilst Boston was off flying. Quite often I sat on the doorstep with a neighbour and we would drink wine and smoke copious amounts of cigarettes together. We found a connection through our isolation of being mothers in the desert and being in distant relationships. I was beginning to notice a pattern that no matter how I tried to find community, in some way I managed to isolate myself.

I was desperate to try and make things work. I had decided he must not be attracted to me, so I tried being super blonde, skinny, brunette, you name it, anything to get his attention. I felt I could have bent over naked in front of the TV and he would tell me to move as I was blocking it. We decided to take our daughter on a family holiday to Scotland so that she could meet all of my extended family from there and we did a driving tour. I'll never forget when we were on that tour, I thought, "oh, we haven't had sex for ages, maybe six or seven weeks." We'd maybe only had it a handful of times through the year, and this was now May 2013. Our daughter "Love" was one.

I remember one night thinking that this could be the night. He'd taken a bottle of red wine into the bedroom. We had this beautiful little Airbnb on a coastal, cold windswept town. There was a log fire and we'd had a beautiful meal. I let him know I was going to hop in the shower to rinse off the day and freshen for our imminent sexy time. I was literally like a minute and when I came back out he was snoring with a glass of wine in his hand. That night I energetically rolled over and closed down, I couldn't take any more rejection. It had broken me. I thought I was the ugliest person in the world, and I believe that subconsciously he was doing this to push me away so that I'd break up with him. I always tried to make it work again, but this time was different and I'd felt it shift.

We had a beautiful trip but it felt more like we were "friends". We got back from the holiday and tried to do another couple of date nights.

One night we were at dinner and I asked him how the chicken was, then thought, "I can't speak to this guy for the next 50 fucking years about the chicken"!! I needed something more, my soul was yearning for something deeper, yearning to have deep discussions about the universe and the meaning of life. I just knew in that moment that I was never going to get it from that man. I had to accept him for who he was and I had to accept that there was nothing wrong with who he was, but he just wasn't compatible with me. We, innately, were not compatible at the deepest level. No matter how we tried, it just didn't work.

Along with counseling, I had tried spicing up our love life to no avail. I was so deprived sexually by this stage it was oozing out of me – unhealthy sexual energy that is. I was fine at ignoring urges and wandering eyes when I was sober but after a few wines I became overtly flirtatious. I needed to get attention elsewhere to feed my insecurities to prove that I still "had it". I am a very committed and loyal person though, so this began to fuck with my head. This kind of behaviour was not in alignment with how I wanted to act in a relationship, but I just wanted my husband to notice me, to want me.

One night I went out with the girls and ended up having a ravenous escapade in a public bathroom with my best friend out there, Louise. I don't quite remember how it started, but all of a sudden she had me pinned up against the wall kissing me with a passion I hadn't felt in years, and ripping my skirt up reaching her hand between my trembling thighs. When we finally finished our make out session, the realisation of what I had done became apparent and I thought the only way to appease my guilt would be for us both to go home and hop into bed with Boston to even the score. In our drunk, not so logical mind this made perfect sense. Everything was fine in the morning – my friendship with Louise remained as strong as ever, in fact I think we went shopping at IKEA. I think it spiced things up for a millisecond with Boston, but it wasn't long before things were as distant as ever before.

One morning I finally built up the courage and said, "I can't do this anymore." Love was down for her morning nap and Boston just walked upstairs, packed a bag and walked out the front door. I began skipping around the living room, feeling this weight lifted off my shoulders. Admittedly that feeling only lasted a little while before the fear and the doubt and all those things came back into play. I know I could've stayed around for a few extra years but that would've made the separation even harder. At this point Love was still young enough not to really know what was happening and the new version of her reality would be her new norm, international co-parenting.

So that was it. I had to begin my plan to move back home. I think deep down there was this rejected little girl inside me that wanted daddy to stay and fight and that's how it played out in my relationship. I wanted my husband to prove my worthiness by staying and fighting for me, but he just didn't have it in him and we didn't really have much to fight for by that stage. At the time I was studying hairdressing in Dubai, so I set myself a goal to complete my training and head towards Bali for a month to regather myself before moving back to Perth. For the first time in about 12 years I had a plan to go and live in Perth because I felt like I needed friends and family around me, and that's what I did. I think I spent the month of July and half of August in Bali trying to re-find myself before I headed back to little old Perth.

CHAPTER EIGHT

BABY AND A BACKPACK

I arrived back in Perth two weeks before my 30th birthday with a one-and-a-bit-year-old baby, and the backpack that I'd left to go traveling with all those years beforehand – although I was a very different version of the girl who'd left all those years before. My six-month plan to make money and go back on the road had become a five-year journey that included marriage, becoming a mother, learning and unlearning everything that I thought I knew about what I wanted in my life, and who I was.

My body had held itself together through all the emotional stress but when I got back to a safe place, it just completely fell apart and all hell broke loose. My skin started breaking out, I was getting perioral dermatitis around my chin, swollen lymph nodes, what felt like chronic fatigue, my adrenals were smashed, and I didn't know which way was up.

When I got back to Perth I moved in with Candy, my life long buddy, for a few months to get back on my feet. It was deeply healing being back around her and the familiarity of my childhood. The first step was to figure out how to get myself set up financially again, so I got back into waitressing topless and nude at private parties on the weekends. This gave me time to be a mum during the week and to be honest I couldn't handle much more than a few nights work. I was an emotional wreck. I began second guessing myself: had I made the right choice? Would I find someone now I was a single mum? The enormity of solo parenting an 18-month-old was overwhelming, I was not prepared for the sleep regression, night terrors, meltdowns and tantrums, and that was just me…only kidding! It was tough. In Abu Dhabi I had a live-in helper who made sure that the house was clean and tidy, that there was healthy food and fresh green juice for everyone daily, and she took care of Love while I studied or had to pop out for something. Life in that aspect had flowed. Here I was with this newfound freedom, but at the same time I felt trapped by my responsibility to this beautiful little girl.

Stripping and being Mercedes again was my outlet, and I loved it. It was my way of interacting with adults, and I had learned by this stage that I wasn't the choo-choo train mum that I thought I'd like to be. I love my daughter dearly, but I can't sit at home and listen to Teletubbies day in, day out, and play dollies. I worked part time as a hairdresser during the week, and during some weekends, Mercedes came back out to play. Mercedes was sassy, Mercedes was fun, and at that time in my life, my real persona was deflated, overwhelmed, insecure, and worthless.

In a way, it was a very big part of my healing. It helped build me back up again. Initially I thought, "Oh, my gosh, I'm too old. I'll never be able to go back." I distinctly remember one night working at a 21st thinking, "Oh my fucking God, they're going to hate me." Instead, they had thought I was only 25 and loved me, so I rolled with it. There was something empowering about really earning my own money again, and in that industry, you get a lot of external validation. I was constantly being told how awesome I was, how pretty I was, how hot I was, and what a great body I had. Slowly but surely it rebuilt me after the rejection from Boston that I had allowed to strip me down. My confidence was starting to come back, but it wasn't from within.

It was yet again based on what I believed about myself from what I was hearing externally. It didn't take much to shake me.

I actually reconnected with my high school sweetheart at my 30th. I was a fair few champagnes deep by this stage so I went over and handed him my thong I had been wearing. No words were needed, he led me by the hand to a cab back to his place, throwing clothes off and stumbling up stairs. We had drunken rockstar sex, all over the house, in every imaginable position. The next morning I presumed we would just end up back together but I had got it so wrong. He was just "having fun".

So here I was, back in Perth. My friends and family were going on about their own lives and I had a massive falling out with my mother. She's never been particularly happy about me being in the industry and she's made that very clear either in silence or in shouting it from the rooftops. She was really disappointed that I hadn't made my marriage

work, because Boston was a good man with a stable job. That's very much the old paradigm – that those two things should have been enough. I guess, to some point, it possibly brought up her own insecurities and unresolved issues around not being able to make her own marriage work. Regardless of the reasons, she decided that she didn't want to support me by looking after Love if I was going to be working in that industry. I can now see it was a misguided attempt of love - to steer me away from the industry as a result of her fear that I would spiral back into drugs, like I had done in my younger years.

So, after a very long, abusive phone call, I sent her a text. This is the first time I really remember standing my ground with my mother. I told her that unless she was going to pay my bills and help support me, she didn't have any right to be commenting on what I was doing to provide for my family, and that though I'd never stop her from seeing her granddaughter, until she could be okay with my work or at the very least not bring it up all the time, then she didn't need to be a part of my life.

We went through a few months with very little contact, and slowly we got back in touch. We just didn't really speak about the topic. So, things were on the up there, but I was realising just how lonely and tough motherhood could be. I feel like a lot of single mothers or mothers with partners that work away can identify with me on this – that once the baby goes to bed at 6:00, and you've cleared the dishes and got set for the next day, it's like, what do you do with yourself?

I sought solace online, chatting to guys, or connecting through Facebook, because I wanted to escape the feelings, the thoughts that I was left with after a busy day. Some of those feelings and thoughts scared me, like that I was 30 and had been put out to pasture. I didn't want to be on my own.

I did find some solace in an amazing new friendship with an incredible woman going through a similar experience. We had been put in touch through my close friend, Louise from Dubai. She said I HAD to connect with her friend in Perth, Michelle, as we would get on like a house on fire. We had both been hesitant to reach out but when she finally did it was a godsend. She got me and I got her. To this day she will never know how much she helped me through this space and how deeply grateful I am for our connection. Women supporting one another really have the capacity to move mountains!

But I still wondered if I could just find another boyfriend and fill the void. Could I do that? Is that possible? I tried that way for a long time, but dating in your 30s is not like it was in your 20s, that's for sure. There's ghosting, there's benching, there's not acting too cool, not being too out there, and these were things that I hadn't learned yet. So, as much as I thought I was ready, I had no idea what I was in for. Whether a toxic fling or empty one night stand dating life was starting to wear down on me. I was told on many occasions that I was having trouble finding a man due to my saucy stripper secret and when my chips were down I believed them.

Although I was in the industry I was only working occasionally, and sometimes I wouldn't work for months on end in the hope I would be saved by my Prince Charming. Yes, I watched many a fairytale when I was a kid. The thing is, nothing changed. At this point, I was really struggling. I was struggling to be single and to be a mum, and I didn't know how to combine the two of them. I actually hold a lot of guilt around not being as present, not physically but mentally, with my daughter during that time.

I was just trying to keep my head above water and do the best that I could do, to earn money and try to figure out what I wanted to do with my life. I was still waiting for this prince on a white horse to come sweep me off my feet and save me from myself. It took a while before I realised that no one else can do that. It was only me. Again, I picked up where I left off spiritually years before. It was like this vortex in Dubai where I had just forgotten a lot of the stuff that I'd learned over the years about presence and manifesting and goal setting and spirituality.

I really started to work on myself again and gain a little further understanding about relationships and things like masculine and feminine energies, and do a lot of reflection. I could see where I went wrong in my marriage, I could see the dynamics and how they played out. I was consistently emasculating this poor man and I thought that that was normal, because it's the only thing I had seen in relationships around me.

In Australia, we show love by taking the piss out of each other, tearing shreds off each other and sarcasm. I started thinking, "Why do we want to do that? Don't we want to build the people that we love up? Why do we want to tear shreds off each other?" My inner journey started to unravel and I was seeing loads of different healers for different things, and I think I made a mistake in digging up too much emotional "stuff" before I could really have time to heal and integrate from the last session.

Probably eight months after I came back, my mum needed a place to stay and I was searching for an Au Pair so, in exchange for rent, she moved in and began helping me with Love. It's probably not the healthiest idea that we've had, but I'm forever grateful for it. I want to make this clear – my mother isn't a bad person by any means, in fact she is funny, charismatic and caring. She just had a different way of showing it that I couldn't see. I didn't help our relationship because at the time, I was unknowingly was carrying so much hurt, blame and resentment towards the way things had turned out in my teen years.

I went into spiritual overload and decided that I no longer wanted to wait. I no longer wanted to wait for the perfect man to come along. I decided to let go of the pressure on myself, the self-imposed pressure to have a nuclear family. I didn't need a man to be complete.

I'd managed to get my own white picket fence, but I still didn't know what I truly wanted to do. I wanted to find the awe again, that feeling I had before. I wanted to find wonder and to marvel at things again. I wanted to feel alive and happy. The only places that I had felt that previously were on the stage and the open road. So, I decided that in January of 2016 I was going to take off with Love, and hit the open road. That's exactly what I did. January 2nd, 2016, Love and I packed up our life with no plan, no itinerary and just a couple of rough bookings, and camped and housesat our way around Australia, New Zealand, and the world.

I was lucky to have made some smart moves with inheritance from my dad, and that allowed me the financial freedom to follow my dreams.

CHAPTER NINE
OUR GYPSY ADVENTURE

Like with any life changing moment, there were nerves, excitement and joy. This new adventure was far more challenging than before. You see, now not only was I responsible for how this trip would affect me, I was responsible for how this would affect my daughter. This was not a fly by the seat of my pants decision, for once. I put lots and lots of thought into it. I researched the effects on children who travel, I spoke to people who had done it, I even found an online community of single parents that were traveling around Australia just like I was going to.

After finding a lot of evidence to support that traveling could have positive effects on a child and with a lot of people reflecting the words, "happy mama, happy baby" back to me, I made my decision. This didn't stop the guilt I was carrying about uprooting my daughter again. You see, I had kind of made it my mission in life to protect her from anything and everything that may add to her initial "abandonment" wound. When I first adopted her I had this stable, happy family plan that would provide her with all the secure attachment and emotional stability she needed after her challenging start to life. Now these were all my projections based on my own life experience and understanding of the effect that it can have later in life, but what I didn't realise was that she may never grow to experience the same issues I had, and through all my well-meaning micro-managing I may have created more anxiety than necessary. I carried so much guilt and stress until I finally realised that she would have to learn her own lessons and maybe this is exactly what she is here to learn! The best I can do is to teach her resilience, love and support her unconditionally.

January 2nd, 2016 rolled around pretty quickly after the decision was made. We loaded up the Kluger with some very basic camping equipment, two chairs, a table, a camp stove, a pan, one each of the essentials, a fork, a knife, a plate, a cup, and a two-man tent with a blow-up mattress. This was what I had reduced my life to. I mean, that and a couple of bags of clothes, and we were on the road.

The first two weeks of the trip didn't feel like we were going anywhere because we were fortunate enough to stay with family friends in Bunbury. My family came down to Bridge Town and we all rented a big beautiful house there and hung out for a few days. Then I drove down to Denmark, where another really good friend of mine and his little daughter came down for the weekend. We hung out and took the girls to the beach, and he had a group of friends down there too. I felt like someone was holding my hand and leading me gently onto this journey. It was much more pleasant than ripping the bandaid off.

I had given myself a little challenge the year prior by taking Love to Italy and backpacking for a month. So many people have reached out to me asking how I did it, how I managed to travel alone with a little one in tow and I always suggest before you commit to a long term plan, to do a medium length trip to really see if it's something you enjoy and to see whether your child is a kind of child who will be able to adapt to being on the road. In Italy I had a pram, a 13-kilo backpack, and a 12-kilo child. Love adjusted beautifully, and it made me feel confident that I could step out on this journey around Australia. Don't get me wrong, there were challenging, tiring moments where I wondered what on earth I was doing! My mum came to meet us for part of the trip and it was actually a really healing time to have us all there on holidays together. I feel it is super important to begin to make new memories and not let our past relationship define us. Again, something easier said than done.

By the time I had said goodbye to my friends in Denmark and arrived in Esperance, I was questioning everything, wondering "Have I made the right decision? Oh my gosh, now I'm with my child 24/7 and no one to help me." I had managed to put my neck out in the process of setting up our campsite one night, so I desperately needed to see a physio or a chiro and thought, "What am I going to do with my daughter?" She's not the kind to sit there quietly while you get massaged or adjusted. It just wasn't in her age range or skillset yet, and even now she struggles to keep quiet. This really drilled home that questioning voice that was again saying, "What the fuck are you doing, you crazy biatch!" I put Love to bed that night and remember sitting there alone with my thoughts feeling overwhelmed and realising that yet again I had that dreaded feeling of isolation. I went to sleep eventually and woke the next morning to an email saying, "Hi, I've read the first page of your blog," because I had started a small Facebook page to keep my family and friends and whoever cared updated on our whereabouts and what we were doing. And I don't know, to this day, how or where she came across it, but a journalist found it and wanted to write a piece about me for The Daily Mail UK.

Now, this had to be a sign from the universe that I was on the money, it was so amazing and really made me trust that I was on the right path just a little bit more. It was like the universe rewarding me for taking action, and the universe always rewards action. Always. There's not a time I can think of, when I've taken right action in line with something that was honouring my soul's journey, and not been rewarded with validation that I am on track.

So there we were, all of a sudden with 3,000 people following us and our adventure. I became inundated with calls, questions and people asking how they could do it. I was stunned to say the least – I didn't really even feel like I had anything to share at that point. Only about 12 days into our trip, what could I possibly have to share? I see now that what I was sharing was hope, possibility and inspiration that travelling solo with a child was achievable! I'd also mentioned in my blog that I was no longer going to be waiting for Prince Charming to save me, and it was an unusual story because of the adoption as well. So, "Mum takes adopted daughter to travel around Australia," were the kind of headlines that were flashing about.

I managed to leverage selling the story to some women's magazines, and made appearances on some TV shows in Melbourne and Sydney. I met my schoolgirl crush, Larry Emdur, and realised very quickly that because I was towering over him, I would never be able to live out my schoolgirl fantasy. Anyway, we were traveling, and it boosted my ego to some extent. And not only my ego, but it reached me on a deeper level because at this point, people would message to let me know how I'd changed their life, just by reading my story. To me, I didn't feel like I was doing anything extraordinary, but in finding my own freedom and sharing about it, I allowed others permission to think outside the box and to think that this was possible for them as well.

After a few days experiencing Esperance and it's AMAZING beaches (if you love beaches, get to Lucky Bay), getting my neck sorted whilst Love was entertained by the receptionist and some supplies we headed off into the "wilderness". Well for me it was the wilderness, having never ventured further than a few hours away from major city by car. As I was driving up this long isolated one-way road, I could see all the black tree stumps on the side of the road, and my pulse started to race and the anxiety began to take over me once again. There had been huge, town-destroying fires throughout the southwest of Western Australia that week, and I began to wonder if I was driving head on into bush fire territory. My breathing was laboured, my thoughts erratic, all while I was trying to play it cool and keep things calm for Love. The next minute, as I was trying to talk myself down off the ledge of paranoia, we see smoldering smoke on the roads. It was incredible to realise that I was the only person who could calm myself down, I was now in charge, and that I didn't have the space to freak out or I would be no help to either of us. I pulled over, trying to get a blip of service to Google the area, but with no luck. I had to get out of my head and come back into my body, tap into my intuition and make a decision on whether to keep going – and that's just what we did, finally reaching the start of the Nullarbor!!

To most of you my panic may seem totally irrational, but for someone who had set their dining room table on fire by accident at a young age it felt, in my body, like a matter of life and death. We are all a result of our collected experiences of childhood. If the first time you encounter something it is a scary or stressful moment, the next time you experience it, even as an adult, will trigger the same emotional response in your body. Until, of course, you can find a deeper level of healing around the trauma.

Got The Life by Korn was my main driving song. I don't think I had heard it since high school and it brought back the feelings of angst and determination in me. I just put it on and jammed away to it. A lot of people asked how I managed to keep Love entertained the whole time, and one answer is that we had A LOT of singalongs…her musical palette ranges across Five, Korn, Classical, RnB and Mowtown. I also had a bit of a process where, during the first two hours of driving, we would do some kind of learning or car game. Then for the next two hours she would usually nap, then after her nap, she'd have a little snack, and then I'd put a movie or something on the laptop for her. This was my process. It was kind of my way of trying to not be solely reliant on technology to keep her entertained, and also a little bit of a system that allowed her to feel like she had routine even when we were on the move. Not all days were this long in the car but I just wanted to get across the Nullabor as quickly as possible. In the height of summer it is not a pleasant place to spend much time!

We spent a week or so recovering with a friend of Candy's in Melbourne who I had met a few times before. We just needed to rest! Who would've thought that driving or sitting down all day could be so painful! My bones felt bruised, and I felt as though my insides would fall out, my entire pelvic area ached – gross I know! But these are things I was totally unprepared for.

Leaving the car in Melbourne, we headed to New Zealand on our first pre-planned stint, at Kiwiburn. If any of you have heard of Burning Man, imagine a grassroots, small-scale version. It's a really free-thinking event. Basically, people are laughing, singing, doing art, dancing, dressing up and acting as though they were without restriction. The ethos is to build community and act in the interest of the community. You can't buy anything and you can't leave behind any trace on the environment. I was lucky enough to have a dear friend, Free, attending and he shared his tiny home with us as accommodation. I had experienced a really deep connection with Free years earlier at a tantra retreat in New Zealand. He was the first person to really see me, someone I felt deep intimacy with simply by staring into his eyes. We both experienced deep healing that week and it was amazing to get to spend time with each other again.

After the festival was over, Love had some time with her great grandfather on her dad's side. My "ex" mother-in-law had flown down to spend some time with Love, her daughter and her dad. This was perfect timing, as always. After six weeks on the road I was ready for a little "break". It was also perfect as Candy (my all time bestie) was in town with her partner's family and I caught up with two of the girls I had lived with in Dubai all those years before! I travelled a lot of the north in NZ and it truly is one of the most stunning places I have ever experienced. Like Scotland and Australia mixed into one. I only seemed to encounter those with a very laid back outlook on life. I highly recommend!

We arrived back in Melbourne and spent some time free camping and housesitting around the state. Camping in National Parks, The Ottways, Warrnambool and many a little town in between. One adventure found us camping at a soon-to-be therapy farm for children with behavioural or physical disabilities. Imagine me going from hair extensions and false nails to hammering in star picket fencing and shitting in the bush! I often giggle to myself about the contrast. I am also proud to know that I can rough it when needed. One particular lady we housesat for a few times in Warrnambool even let us stay when she got back from her holidays as we got along so well. To this day, my daughter still mentions her. To me, it feels like there's all these special, beautiful people who feel like family scattered all over the globe.

After Melbourne came Bali. We needed some sunshine and I wanted to do my yoga teacher training. We lined things up so that Boston was in Bali to have time with Love and so that I could attend my classes. This was a lot more difficult than we anticipated. Love wanted me all the time, and I felt guilty and stretched emotionally between a demanding course and the demands of a three-year-old.

Halfway through I contracted dengue fever, which was actually one of the most horrific things that I've ever experienced in my life. The stress had weakened my immune system so I had nothing left when it came to recovering. It was as if had been driven over by a steamroller, like every bone in my body was broken and I ached from head to toe. I spent the next few weeks slowly recovering and trying to mother full time again – with Boston now gone I had no option. Candy flew over to meet me for a pre-planned holiday, but I had limited spouts of energy in between manic bouts of paranoia and anxiety about getting sick again, and the idea of Love possibly getting dengue sent me into a tizz.

After staying and recouping there for a while, we headed back to Melbourne just in time to meet my Mum who flew in for Love's 4th birthday. We had a great few days and she went horseriding for the day! Mum left and we hit the road again, visiting friends and friends of friends along the way. My aim was to get to the Sunshine Coast where my mother-in-law lived. My body was not recovering well and simple things were taking it out of me. It was awesome to stay there a few weeks, eat well, sleep well and have some help looking after a now very active now four-year-old! I am forever grateful for the help that Boston's mum and sister provide with Love. I couldn't manage without it.

With the top end of Australia heading into wet season and not feeling like I was an experienced enough driver to navigate the dirt roads and possible flooding I felt it best to redirect our trip. I posted on Facebook to see if anyone was traveling in Europe. Again, the universe guided me to a beautiful man who had couch surfed at our house the year before. He was going to be hitchhiking around Europe. So in exchange for some help driving and caring for Love I offered to rent a campervan and he set his tent up outside. He was from Holland so we met him there and set to planning our journey. We travelled through Holland, France and Geneva before heading to the UK.

In the UK I got to meet up with many of my closest friends from Dubai and their families. We got to spend some quality time with Michael, Stella and their gorgeous son for the first time since the adoption. Some days it was hard going and isolating, while other days were full of awe, wonder, joy and connectedness. I often oscillated between extreme highs and enormous lows. We both began to get sick of moving around. I started craving normal things. I wanted a routine. The little gypsy soul in me no longer wanted to go on massive missions – I wanted to have a place to call home.

CHAPTER TEN

SUPERCHARGE YOUR STORY

So, after doing a little trip around Scotland to visit my family, I decided it was time to head back to Perth. We settled in a place where I thought that I would find my tribe, near Fremantle. Being that little bit of a gypsy, hippy wanderer, I thought that maybe I'd find my peeps there. Much to my dismay, I recreated my pattern of isolation. I thought, "How have I done this again?" All of my friends lived about 45 minutes north, and I really limited myself being down there because I didn't know very many people. This time, my depression got really bad. I felt like I was a caged lion. I would pace at night, and although I'd never even contemplated the idea of suicide, I was having thoughts about it. Never anything that I would carry out, but I could strongly identify with the feeling of just wanting to make this feeling go away. This feeling was so intense at times that I didn't know what to do with myself. I would say that it's one of the most emotionally challenging spaces that I've ever been in.

After being through divorce, drug use, and losing a parent I thought I had made it through the worst, but this was next level. In fact, it was possibly even worse as it had no apparent root cause, just a deep feeling of dissatisfaction. No amount of yoga and meditation could shift it. I decided that, again, only I was in charge of my life and only I had the power to change my reality. I tuned into myself and asked where I needed to go or be. I had a deep calling that I needed to go to Bali, so after nine months in Perth, I moved to Bali and my newfound best friend Chloe came over to help me transition. Seriously, that woman is a godsend. She has had my back from day one and supported everything that I've ever done. I'd like to take this moment to mention how grateful I am and how important it is to nurture good friendships and treat them like relationships. Quite often we can take them for granted, but when all your chips are down, they're the people who are there for you. I truly have met some amazing women in my life and they all know who they are.

Coming back to the story, I was in Bali and had enough inheritance left to stay for a year and a half, but I hoped to find a way to earn and stay there more long term. It took me a while to get settled, and I moved around a lot to try to find the right villa. About nine months into being there, after dating a few guys in town and nothing really working out, I started seeing this guy around at all these random places. There would be no one else at a particular restaurant and said guy would walk in. I had also seen him at the school, one of the dad's so I just presumed that he was married, and that was that. About two months later, we were given an official introduction by one of the other dads at school. And he very quickly made it known that he was not married and asked me and Love to spend some time with him and his two kids on the weekend.

He was a charismatic French man who had the gift of the gab. He adored me in the way that no one had in a long time. Again, I had my checklist of things that I thought that I wanted or needed, and he checked off the criteria. One of my major shortcomings is the fact that, because I'm such a woman of my word, I believe that everyone else has the same value. He told me all these things that I wanted to hear about communication and conscious-relating, and I just thought, "Yes. Amazing. This man that gets it!" So I dove straight in, wanting to believe all the things I was hearing.

We had an amazing holiday to Uganda together. It was my third time there and I was volunteering with my newfound skills that I had acquired during my study to be a Doula. I found a birthing home in the middle of Luwero, Uganda, where I spent some time while the Frenchman travelled and kayaked on the Nile. I had done this before and wasn't interested in going again, so it worked perfectly. We reunited, hired a 4WD with a rooftop tent and went on safari. We went to Murchison Falls, spent the night in a rhino sanctuary and trekked with them – it was mind blowing. We had such a great time, and it really cemented my feelings towards him.

As we headed back towards Luwero, we experienced a really scary moment. We found ourselves trapped in a town where there was unrest between the local motorbike taxi drivers and the authorities. We were in the car and I could sense something was wrong when we stopped in the line of traffic. There was debris all over the roads, everyone was standing lining the streets, and we had ended up stuck in the traffic outside a local watering hole, which made me nervous. A group of drunk men began shouting Mzungu, Mzungu (white person) and jumping on the side of the car, shaking it from side to side. I am pretty sure it was in jest, but my heart was in my mouth. I didn't feel safe. I screamed at Frenchie to turn around, and we did about a one million-point turn and headed back to a petrol station we had seen upon entry to the town. I was so shaken, my nervous system was buzzing with fear.

We had some food and chatted with other locals that were also seeking shelter. We found out it was a stand to support a local motorbike taxi driver who had been jailed for not having the correct papers. We were in a café next to the petrol station laughing and playing cards while we waited for the trouble to pass, and next thing we knew there was riot police and tear gas everywhere. We were instructed to lock the café door, take cover and try not to inhale the gas, terrifying to say the least. As quickly as the situation arose, it was cleared and we were given news by someone at the café that it was now safe to pass. I was so freaked out that I asked a local to come in the car with us to see that we got safely to the other side. This majestic older woman obliged and we got through without any trouble. Although nothing happened in the end, it was enough to have me shaken for days!! We enjoyed another week travelling Uganda and then headed back to Bali to get the kids back from their respective other parents!

We spent the next few months alternating between our two houses, trying to cram five of us into two bedrooms at each place. It was very unsettling for everyone as we didn't have set dates, and I felt this whirlwind feeling whenever I was around him. Chaos tended to follow him everywhere, and now it followed me too. I had come to a place in life where I valued organisation and quiet, zen-like surroundings. I had myself an amazing bottom floor in a mansion that backed onto a jungle ravine, complete with an infinity pool. Around the same time both of our leases were up and we each had to find something else. Along the way we had been open to the idea of moving together had we found the right place.

We moved into a big, beautiful, turquoise blue house, in the middle of the rice fields. I had actually been doing a manifestation journal of my life at the time and only weeks earlier I had described almost that exact house! I was so excited to move into my "dream" house and have all the kids together and provide that wholesome family feeling I had longed for as a child and that I so desperately wanted for Love. Very quickly, however, I began to see that although he understood the concepts he had spoken about when we first met, about conscious relating and communication on a logical level, he hadn't quite figured out how to embody it. Instead of those feelings of joy and happiness, I began to panic. I couldn't access him anymore on an emotional level. It was like the moment we moved in he pulled the plug and got busier and busier with work and life.

The kids began to act out with the new dynamics and, although we attempted to be as present as possible, it became harder and harder the busier he got. Then the harder it got, the busier he got. I know situations are never 100% one sided and I am sure I played a role of my own in the dynamic not working too. There was barely enough time for him to be there for himself and his kids, let alone me and Love. I was tired of being squeezed in and Love barely being looked up at from his laptop when she spoke, and even after many long discussions and promises of change, nothing seemed to shift. I had been avoiding, once again, the knowledge that this was not the right fit.

Prior to moving in I thought, "Wow, this is the ending of the book that I want to write because I've found "the one" and I'm living my best life, in the middle of the rice fields, and this is what everyone wants with their life, right?" I'm sad to say that no, it wasn't my ending and he wasn't my one. After much communication on my side he told me that he just wasn't ready and that he didn't have the time to put in to our relationship. I moved out again, another relationship over just before my birthday. I moved out and got my own place, where suddenly it dawned on me, do you know what? I had found the ending of my book! I had found the true love I had been searching for all along and that I had in fact had her with me all along…it was ME!

That was really the truest and greatest birthday gift that I could have received. Embracing who I was on the deepest level and knowing my value. Relationships are tough. For some reason, we think it's going to be easy if it's the right one. It's not going to be easy. Anything that is worthwhile is challenging – childbirth, studying to become a doctor, running a marathon, climbing Kilimanjaro, these are all things that take extreme dedication, extreme hard work, but they're all worthwhile. That is what we need to start selling as a framework around relationships, rather than the fact that it should be easy. Now, you have to find your own boundaries in what you are willing to put into a relationship, you still have to honour yourself and know when you are flogging a dead horse.

When both people are willing to meet in the middle, then it can work. If you're constantly picking up more than your partner's end of the slack, then both people aren't equally investing. You only get out what you put in, and one person can't carry a relationship. There needs to be two people who want to work on it. This wasn't the case for my relationship with the charismatic Frenchman. My lesson here was realising it fairly soon and honouring myself enough to know when to walk away. I deserved more than words and false promises, and so did my daughter. I felt hurt, betrayed and disillusioned, but I also knew I hadn't worked this hard to settle for less. Making the hard decision to leave turned out to be one of the most empowering choices of my journey.

With my savings dwindling and my relationship over I felt an extreme pull to leave Ubud. There I was giving up what I thought what was going to be my "ideal" life in Bali, and at the same time finding the true love I had been searching the world for, right there inside of me. My travels were not in vain – they helped me to access that part inside of me by opening my heart to adventure, meeting the most amazing people, experiencing challenge, isolation and different cultures and seeing life through different eyes. Each adventure brought me closer to my inner truth. I'd heard this so many times before. We've all heard it said that, "No one will love you unless you love yourself." It took me many great attempts to love myself. I saw many healers, meditated, did yoga, sought to "fix" all my flaws to become more loveable to both myself and the world around. In the end I realised that I had to totally love myself as I was…or at least show myself compassion when I didn't feel like the best version of myself. We all have darkness. When compassion and acceptance can be found in where we are, it's then that we can truly evolve and strive for more.

I flew back to Perth in November of 2018 with a spring in my step, instead of my tail between my legs. There was a part of me that thought, "Ugh, I'm going to have to go back to work," was I going to feel that judgement again? Was I going to run the story, "What am I doing with my life?" I was 35. I'd always made these promises to myself that I'd leave the industry by 28, I'd leave by 30, I would never be doing it at 32, and yet here I was back on the bones of my ass, and starting in the industry again.

I got straight back into busy season and I realised how much I had missed it. I hadn't stripped in clubs for years now, having instead worked at private parties, bucks nights, golf days and poker nights. For me, I find this a much better way of earning than the club. I can choose when I am available and manage my own diary, I know that when I am booked I am set to earn a minimum amount without needing to "hustle" and I enjoy the fact that I don't have to get too up close and personal with the clientelle. My job now entails me being more like a party hostess/waitress, I am there to liven things up, to have fun and interesting conversations and of course be easy on the eye. Occasionally I skimpy barmaid at pubs and do strip shows for birthdays and bucks nights too. I began to realise that this lit me up. I felt joyful. I felt like I was myself. And you know what else? I'm really bloody good at it. Sure enough, like in any job, some days are better than others but on the whole I see this as a positive influence. Now I mix my spiritual learnings in with what I bring to my job, I have deeper conversations with people, I attract amazing clients that reflect back my energy, I share about my travels and learnings, I take lessons from clients I interact with...some of the most "spiritual" messages have come from the unbecoming barfly at the end of the bar. I am so grateful for the men that I work for on many levels, I have met some clients that have become friends that are now my biggest supporters. I have made many life long friends from this industry including Perth's Best Girls owner Nat, who revolutionised the industry. She and a team of women that wanted to see women running their own show went to war, eventually running the sleazy agencies out of town. We now have a huge freelance network of boss babes - meaning no middle man, higher standards of girls, higher rates, lower commissions and flexibility to self promote.

Interestingly enough, now that I have reached fuck everybody else land, from a really soft empowered space, I feel ready to transition into whatever is next for me. It's almost like when you accept where you are then your life starts nudging you on to the next thing. I have also, from this space of self-acceptance, attracted the most incredible accepting man into my life. He has my back 150%, we have amazing communication and work at our relationship daily, remembering that it is an honour and a choice to be together. During this transition my relationship with my mum has transformed and is the best it has been in years, for which I feel truly blessed.

After studying tantra, Reiki, yoga, life coaching, the art of communication and learning a shitload from my own life experiences I am now hell bent on bringing love and communication to the world. This begins with loving thyself and THEN bringing it to all your interactions. When you give yourself the time and space to look inward and see what subconscious beliefs have been running your life until this point, it is transformational! Sometimes you just need to be shown your story in another light, to reframe a story you have been telling yourself or listening to others tell you, give your inner critic a new positive script or to start seeing the impossible as I'M POSSIBLE. You may not be aware that you have something holding you back from truly loving who you are and allowing yourself to live the life you desire, yet you can identify with the feeing of being "stuck" or wanting more from life than the material.

I find the best way to do this is through a very simple process.

ALIGNMENT –

Have a good look at all the areas in your life where you are either in or out of alignment. Maybe it's in many areas and maybe it's one major area that then creates a knock-on effect to other areas of your life. Look at your integrity around what you are doing – does it feel right, is it a means to an end or are you avoiding a certain area of your life? It can be challenging but it's really important in change to know where you are starting from.

AWARENESS –

Look at the reasons or beliefs that may be causing imbalance in your alignment. Simply shining the light of awareness on it can be enough to shift things, but some beliefs, guilts or shames need to be looked at a little deeper and in that case may need the assistance of a healer, counsellor or coach.

Once you start to shine awareness on this issue that's your first step – being conscious of whatever it is that's holding you back. We can all have these different stories, and we don't realise until we really sit down and get real with ourselves, and take a look inside. A way to access this at home is the following:

EXERCISE –

- Find a quiet space to sit, bring a journal and pen nearby
- Close your eyes and gently begin to focus on your breathing
- Set an intention for that specific meditation or simply just see what is alive in you at that moment
- Allow each breath to lengthen and relax you – some people work better with relaxing music in the background
- Drop any tension from the shoulder with each exhale
- Begin to scan the body and ask yourself how you are really feeling in that moment – allow yourself to get vulnerable
- Allow the emotion to be and tune in to where it is coming from. Quite often you will know the next step

We are multi-facteted, multi-layered beings. The subconscious holds onto things to help keep us safe. As humans instead of processing our emotions each time they occur we collect them and carry them around with us, unknowingly adding a little at a time to our sacks over the years. When starting to unpack that sack on a healing journey you can expect similar. Your subconscious will show just enough to heal for now and something related may come up later when you are emotionally capable of healing that little bit more.

I wish we could be more like deer. They experience something traumatic and will literally stand up and shake it off, helping it to be processed for the nervous system and left there in the moment! You never see a deer carrying baggage!

This "baggage" we can collect as humans can be a result of anything from really traumatic events to simple misunderstandings that have greatly impacted our lives. I remember recently I ran into a guy from high school. It was like the minute he saw me he couldn't wait to offload this thing that he'd been carrying for years. He said "Oh my gosh. I'm so sorry that I said something racist to your best friend in high school. Do you know I never came back to the school after that day? I was so embarrassed about what I'd said at that party." He went on to explain that he had no idea where that comment had come from as he didn't even feel that way, that he had felt embarrassed about being rejected and reacted with an aim to hurt her back.

The next time I spoke to my bestie I said, "Oh by the way, I ran into Peter from high school, he wanted me to apologise for what happened."

"What the fuck?" she replied. "I don't even remember that happening." This event had been festering under the surface for years for Peter. Sometimes we're carrying guilt and shame for things no one even remembers. How much do you allow how another human perceives you to shape your reality?

ACCEPTANCE –

Accepting where we are at is the best way to embrace change. It creates a driving force or motivation to initiate lasting change. With acceptance we find out that there are things that we may not be able to change, but we can change the way we see them. A story that I had carried for a long time was that men always leave. This story comes from a long line of men that work away or at sea in my family. I had, as a result, recreated this on some level with my relationships – the men in my life would either physically or emotionally leave me. After seeing a coach to help me improve each area of my life I was able to see that though my dad was away, it was not because he wanted to be. He was away because he was working to support our family. In that moment of realisation I managed to flip my story from 'men always leave' to 'men provide and create security for me'. When I changed my internal dialogue the calibre of men that began showing up in my life was like chalk and cheese. I now have a life surrounded by great men, great male friends and an amazing partner. My relationship with existing men that were already in my life has changed too – It's all in the reframe.

ANNIHILATE –

Use coaching processes to destroy the old beliefs and then replace them with new positively framed statements. If you are trying this at home you can start with a simple reframing exercise. Simply write a list of the statements you see flying about your head. Your inner critic can be a nasty one! Mine looked a little like this.

"You're a shit human."

"You're an awful mother."

"You don't deserve it."

Could you imagine talking to someone like this out loud? I was always super nice and compassionate to others but this was my own internal dialogue. Is it any wonder I was struggling to find self-love and self-acceptance? Chances are you have some nasty statements flying around your head. After identifying them, look to reframe that statement in a positive light. Always begin with an "I AM now," so that you are running the show and not your inner critic!

"I am a loving, compassionate and kind human."

"I am the best mother I can be in each moment."

"I am worthy of love and I am enough."

Now take your new statements and plaster them everywhere. Repetition is key in helping you embody these new beliefs. I record mine and listen to them, my friend writes hers on the bathroom mirror, I have a client that pins them on the back of the toilet door!! Whatever works for you! Recite these daily to yourself. At first they may seem like foreign words coming from your tongue but before long you will start to feel them!

ACTION PLAN –

Sit and write yourself a list of things to do. Prioritise what you feel is of most importance. Set short and long term goals for each section of your life. Make this list achievable and short! The point of these goals is to guide yourself in the direction you want to be heading in. Once you can hit these achievable goals the dopamine receptors in your brain light up, creating positive neural pathways and making you want to do this again! What doesn't work is overloading your plate – how do I know this, you ask? Because this was me! A ridiculously high achiever, but when I feel overwhelmed, what triggers in me is shutdown mode. I will look at the overall enormity of a project and do sweet fuck all! Whereas when I break it into bite-sized pieces, it's far more manageable. Even writing this book, I gave myself loads of small deadlines that fit into the overall deadline for the entire book.

Your list could look a little like the following:

Friends & Family

- Schedule extended family dinners once a month
- Leave work early on Fridays to take the kids to the park
- Lock in golf with John twice a month

Personal Growth

- Meditate for five minutes daily
- Journal and reflect on my day
- Recite positive affirmations

Health

- Walk in nature two times a week
- Gym three times a week
- Prepare good meals for the week ahead

Fun/Recreation

- Watch standup comedy once a month
- Go to a food festival
- Dance around the house twice a week

Romance

- Go on three dates this month (if single)
- Have a weekly date night or time frame just for you two to have fun (if in a couple)
- Have a technology free evening together to just be

Finances

- Consolidate debt
- Save for a holiday
- Clear bills as soon as they come in

Career

- Apply for that promotion (even if it scares you)
- Apply yourself fully when at work
- Up-skill yourself in the industry

ACTIVATE

Activating is the doing part of your action plan! It's now time to execute things in your life, showing steadfastness to embody the updated version of you. See this healing as a software upgrade! Regular upgrading helps us to avoid those toxic little bugs that start to interfere with the system.

The saying "Rome wasn't built in a day" is true! But the right action was taken daily to achieve the feat. Break down your action plan and implement things little by little. Maybe choose two topics a months and tick off the goals until they become second nature and then add some more. This will ensure your changes are sustainable.

One foot in front of the other, it's okay if your goals change, it's okay to be open to where life is guiding you so long as you are on the path and walking it.

A simple thing that can shift things in the blink of an eye is GRATITUDE, even when you are in a situation that feels like you have nothing to be grateful for. It could be a warm home, a job, an amazing family and the ability to focus on the good. This is not to ignore or discount the "bad" or hurtful situations you may be going through, but more to help you shift your vibe and attract more good into your life.

Some of the times the way that I have gotten myself out of my deepest funks has literally to been to get out of my own way, get the fuck over myself and go and help somebody who is in a worse situation. There's something deeply humbling in doing that because I always find that they're helping me just as much as I'm helping them.

Here we are. It seems like we're reaching the end of the book, a huge feat I once thought impossible. Fortunately I had amazing coaches help me to break it down into achievable pieces. YES even coaches have coaches, we all have blindspots or parts of ourselves that we can't access on our own. I can't tell you how grateful I am for everyone who has read or bought a copy and truly wish you all the best on your healing journey. I know you are on one just because you have read this. As humbly as I could possibly say this, I'm fucking awesome, and so are fucking you.

The love that we are all searching for is us xxx

OFFERS

I really believe that everyone deserves a helping hand and access to deeper joy in this human experience. Are you ready to experience this? Well, below I have a gift for you to show my deepest gratitude for you taking the time to read my story.

HOW TO GET MORE MERCEDES!

1. Would you like to reach a deeper sense of self-acceptance and authenticity?

LOVE THYSELF - 5 Steps to Develop a Deeper Sense of Self
LOVE THY NEIGHBOUR – 3 Tips for Communicating Clearly and Consciously (in any relationship not just couples)
Email for your FREE copy

2. Would you like to bring your authentic self in to your everyday interactions??

45 Minute Mentoring
LOVE THYSELF or LOVE THY NEIGHBOUR
Just $99 instead of $299
(limited spaces)

3. Would you like to inspire your workplace, social group to access a deeper sense of self?

To learn effective ways, to set boundaries and communicate clearly from an authentic space?

For a fun, interactive, life-changing event hire Mercedes as a speaker or MC!

Please email mercedesmichaelsinc@gmail.com and explain which option you would like! FREE PDF, MENTORING or SPEAKER.

SPEAKER BIO

Mercedes is a Lover, Mother, Author, Mentor and Action Taker. With a huge open heart and the tenacity to believe in her dreams she inspires others to achieve theirs. Whether in her coaching practice, her personal relationships or in her work environment she strives to be her best and bring out the best in others.

As well as being a Love and Communication Coach, Tantric Practitioner and Business Woman, Mercedes has worked in and out of the stripping industry for 18 years! Finally at peace with who she is, she inspires those who cross her path and gives them permission to fully own their story too!

By fully owning and accepting who you are at the deepest level ANYTHING is possible!

OWN YOUR STORY – LOVE THYSELF

- Flip your story and own your narrative!
- Reframe your picture.
- Access a deeper level of self acceptance.

SEX COMMUNICATION

- The art of saying NO, but giving them a YES!
- How clear communication can lead to better sex and more pleasure
- The Art of Listening deepening connection!

LOVE THY NEIGHBOUR

- Communication in relationship
- Decoding the opposite sex
- Play together, stay together
- Radical Honesty - Growth

Side Note: The affliction we have as a society is wanting it all now! The blue pill approach, even when it comes to healing. We want to be fixed NOW! Immediately. I did just that, I went to every course, healer, medicine man, and psychic you could possibly find in an attempt to be better NOW! I actually "dug" up way more than I was mentally able to cope with at that place and time, which sent me into a spin. I don't say this to scare you, I only say this as I want to really support those on this journey. Looking inwards can bring up all sorts of things and always best to approach from a stable grounded place. Slow and steady wins the race.

ACKNOWLEDGMENTS

Thank you to all the people that have helped me along the journey, the amazing team at Ultimate 48hour Author for helping me actualise this idea, friends and family that have shown me so much love and support in the process. I hope you have enjoyed my story.

To the amazing self expressed boss babes in this industry! From lawyers, doctors, mother's, to savvy business women!

IMAGES

Cover Image – by Robert Moore

Insta @robertmoorecreative

Website www.robertmoorecreative.com

Chapter Ten Image of me – short brunette
INSTAGRAM: @shootwithbrodie
WEB: www.shootwithbrodie.com

Chapter 10 Images – long blonde
@charliesurianophotgrapaher

www.ingramcontent.com/pod-product-compliance
Lightning Source LLC
Chambersburg PA
CBHW021441080526
44588CB00009B/631